'HOOS 'N' HOKIES
THE RIVALRY

100 YEARS OF VIRGINIA/ VIRGINIA TECH FOOTBALL

By Doug Doughty and
Roland Lazenby

Jack Smith
Publisher, Director, Fine Books

Bob Snodgrass
Publishing Consultant

Craig Hornberger
Photo Editor

Jeanne Warren
Editor

Lenore B. Corey
Design and Typography

Original artwork by Andy Kavulich
Dust Jacket Fiber Optic photo Wolf Photography and Chris Dennis
Dust Jacket Design by Randy Breeden
Contributing Photographers: Chris Dennis, Chris Vleisides, John Atkins, Ruth Babylon, Michael Bailey, Sim Carpenter, Gene Dalton, Pete Emerson, Matt Gentry, Jon Golden, David Greene, Dan Grogan, Julie Heywood, Bob Hines, Holsinger Studios, Dave Knachel, Alan Lesse, Walker Nelms, Mark Nystrom, Ed Rosenberry, Frank Selden, Bill Setliff, Cary Shelton, Jamie Stanek, Ralph Thompson Select photos courtesy AP Worldwide Photos,
Remaining photos courtesy the University of Virginia and Virginia Tech athletic departments

Published by Taylor Publishing Company, Dallas, Texas

ISBN: 0-87833-116-6 (General)
ISBN: 0-87833-117-4 (Limited)
ISBN: 0-87833-118-2 (Collectors)

CONTENTS

ACKNOWLEDGMENTS 8
Authors' Dedication

FOREWORD 10
Coaches' Comments

INTRODUCTION 12
The Rivalry

PART I - EARLY TIMES 13
By Roland Lazenby

CHAPTER 1 14
First Blood

CHAPTER 2 28
Heckled by Fate

CHAPTER 3 46
Bulletproof and Beyond

CHAPTER 4 56
Guepe's Merchants

CHAPTER 5 66
Hokies High

CHAPTER 6 78
The Sixtysomething Simmer

PART II - BIG TIMES 92
By Doug Doughty

CHAPTER 7 94
The Resumption

CHAPTER 8 114
State of Flux

CHAPTER 9 140
The Call

CHAPTER 10 166
The Knockout

ACKNOWLE

DOUG DOUGHTY

I want to thank many people including my wife, Beth; and children, Allison, Carrie and Michael. *The Roanoke Times* executive editor, Frosty Landon; managing editor, Bill Warren; sports editor Bill Bern, and sports columnist, Jack Bogaczyk. University of Virginia head football coach George Welsh; assistant coach Rick Lantz; former head coaches Dick Bestwick, George Blackburn and Sonny Randle; former players Mike Brancati, Chip Mark, Charles McDaniel and Elton Toliver; ticket manager/baseball coach Dennis Womack; and sports publication director Craig Hornberger. Virginia Tech athletic director Dave Braine; head football coach Frank Beamer; assistant coach Billy Hite; administrative assistant John Ballein; former head coaches Jerry Claiborne and Bill Dooley; former assistant athletic director Bill Matthews; ticket manager Tom McNeer; former players Bruce Arians, Mickey Fitzgerald, Jimmy Whitten, Steve Johnson, Carter Wiley and Cam Young; current player George DelRicco, and Phil Elmassian, who was an assistant coach at both schools.

ROLAND LAZENBY

First, I would like to thank my wife, Karen, and three children, Jenna, Henry, and Morgan, who put up with the insane deadlines of my work.

DGMENTS

Secondly, several people are responsible for this book coming into being. Jack Smith and Bob Snodgrass at Taylor Publishing saw its value and supported it, as did Steve Horton and Peggy Morse at Virginia Tech and Wood Selig at Virginia.

The research was a critical factor, and Robert Viccellio, Craig Hornberger and Chris King all helped immensely, from digging up old articles to finding just the right photos. There were people on staff at both universities who helped tremendously. At Virginia, the entire sports information staff was a big help, including Director Rich Murray, Associate Director Doyle Smith, Assistant Director Michael Colley and secretary Darlene Craig. I also want to thank University of Virginia Archivist Edmund Berkeley, Jr., and the entire staff of the special collections department at Alderman Library.

At Virginia Tech, the sports information staff of Jack Williams, Dave Smith, and Ed Moore and Director of Sports Marketing Tim East were very supportive and helpful. I also want to thank the special collection archivists at Tech's Newman Library. At *The Roanoke Times*, we owe thanks to executive editor Frosty Landon, managing editor Bill Warren, sports editor Bill Bern, sports columnist Jack Bogaczyk and the entire staff of the Sports Department.

Last of all, I want to thank sweet Ann Wiggins at Taylor Publishing Company, who always makes the work go easier.

VIRGINIA

McCue Center
Post Office Box 3785
Charlottesville, Virginia
22903

Football Coaches Office

804-982-5900
Fax: 804-982-5925

Football Fans,

I would like to thank all of you for your interest in a book that represents a milestone that the University of Virginia is proud to have reached — 100 years of football versus Virginia Tech. I hope you all enjoy the book as much as I have enjoyed coaching against the Hokies for the last 13 years.

In all my years of coaching, only the Army-Navy rivalry comes close to generating the type of intensity on and off the field that occurs during the Virginia-Virginia Tech football game. It is a testimony to college football to have this type of ongoing series that means so much, not only to the players, but to everyone in the state. I am proud to have participated in this series over the last decade. I look forward to the upcoming games and coaching the players that will give their all to make this rivalry what it is, a great tradition.

Sincerely,

George Welsh
Head Football Coach
University of Virginia

Virginia Tech
VIRGINIA POLYTECHNIC INSTITUTE
AND STATE UNIVERSITY

Department of Athletics

Football Office
Jamerson Athletic Center
Blacksburg, Virginia 24061-0502
(703) 231-6368

Football Fans,

Without question, the Virginia Tech-Virginia football game is the top sports event in the Commonwealth each year. The series has produced a thrill-a-minute since the Hokies and Cavaliers first kicked off in 1895. I've been involved as both a player and a coach and know how much the game means to fans all over Virginia.

Veteran sports writers Doug Doughty and Roland Lazenby have done a remarkable job of capturing the magic of the series. Don't miss this blow-by-blow description of one of college football's greatest rivalries.

Sincerely,

Frank Beamer

Frank Beamer
Virginia Tech Head Coach

A Member of the Big East Football Conference

Boston College
University of Miami

University of Pittsburgh
Rutgers

Syracuse Univer...
Temple Univer...

THE RIVALRY

Oklahoma-Nebraska. Ohio State-Michigan. Army-Navy. Harvard-Yale. What makes memorable—even notorious—football rivalries?

For some it's tradition. Others boast prominent programs. Indiana and Purdue award the annual winner the Old Oaken Bucket as a symbol of a hard-fought rivalry.

The football programs at the University of Virginia and Virginia Tech might not be on the order of Ohio State or Michigan, their rivalry might not have the tradition of Army-Navy or Harvard-Yale, and it might not award the annual winner a trophy, but over the last twenty-five years, no college football series has been more competitive. Since 1969, Virginia has won twelve times, Virginia Tech has won twelve times, and there has been one tie.

Could it get any closer? Maybe. Tech holds a slight overall edge at 37-34-5. These numbers, however, don't reveal the spirit, the raw emotion, that color this story.

To understand this rivalry, we must go back 100 years, to an age when football was anything but a good-natured game . . .

Part I - Early Times

By Roland Lazenby

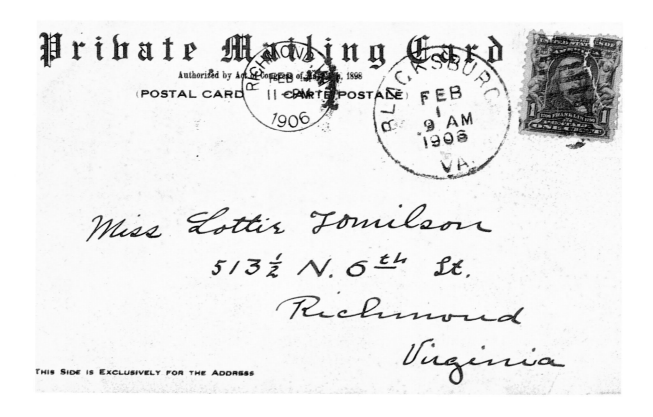

A jubilant Virginia Tech fan needles a UVa compatriot nearly three months after the Hokies' first-ever victory over the Wahoos.

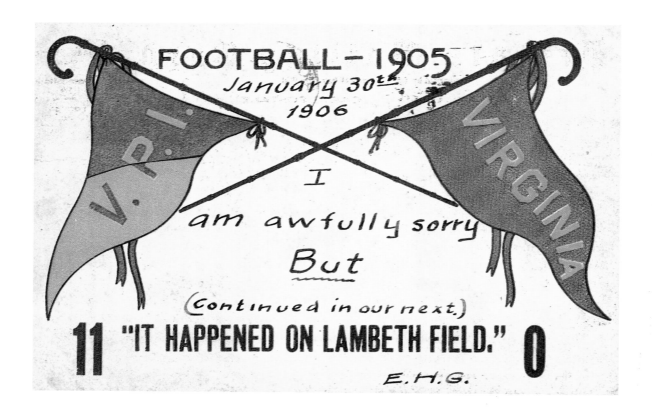

FIRST BLOOD

"Blacksburg has come and gone—gone way back to their seats in the mountains, having taken their licking with about the same grace as the small boy receives castigation."

—*University of Virginia College Topics*
November 19, 1902

From the start, it was more than just a football game, more than just Wahoos vs. Hokies. It was class warfare, Virginia style. A clash of backgrounds and pedigrees. The sons of bankers vs. the sons of farmers. Haughty fraternity boys vs. stone-faced cadets.

It was bluebloods vs. bumpkins.

The bumpkin part of the equation would be Virginia Tech, known back in the old days as Virginia Agricultural and Mechanical College. Heck, the Hokies were so country they used a plow to mark off their first playing field. And when opponents wanted to tweak 'em, they'd bring out signs that read, "Kill the Farmers!"

Actually, the Wahoos were happy just to ignore them.

After all, the "University" had its reputation to uphold. It was Mr. Jefferson's intellectual village, a place of statues and colonnades, a symbol of that old Vir-

Floyd "Hard Times" Meade served as Tech's unofficial mascot in the early years. (Photo VT Special Collections)

ginia aristocracy, a center of law, medicine and—well, snobbery. The Wahoos fancied themselves the natural opponents of Princeton and Penn. In those days, the Ivy League schools were the powers of college football, and playing them confirmed a certain status for Virginia.

When the Hokies approached them back in the 1890s about playing a game, the Wahoos didn't exactly jump at the idea. In fact, they weren't even sure of Tech's correct name, so they referred to it as Blacksburg College, that place way up there in the sticks.

Finally, in 1895, after the Hokies had hired three former Wahoos as coaches, Virginia agreed to play— but only if the Hokies would travel to Charlottesville. Under the circumstances, it didn't take long for a healthy contempt to build between the two, a contempt that would be passed down from generation to generation.

The 1901 VPI squad produced a record of 7-1, its most successful season to that point. The only blemish on the Hokie slate was a disappointing 16-0 loss to UVa.

"Those boys from Virginia always seemed to have a little too much blue in their blood," recalled Mac McEver, who played and then coached at Tech for nearly six decades.

"It's true," agreed Dr. John Risher, a 1932 Virginia grad and longtime Wahoo fan. "I remember going up to Blacksburg for a game, and going into town we saw a field full of cows, and someone pointed and said, 'There's the student body.'"

This kind of one-upmanship is fairly common in college football. Texas vs. Texas A&M. Michigan vs. Michigan State. Wherever there's an esteemed state university and a hungry land grant school, the chemistry brews up a rivalry.

Yet in the Old Dominion, the distinctions were more harshly drawn. Maybe it was the shadow cast by Mr. Jefferson himself. Whatever the reason, the blood ran a little bluer in Charlottesville, and the clods hopped a little higher in Blacksburg. "Our teams were always made up of a lot of prep school graduates, and the Hokies were made up of high school graduates," observed Risher. "We'd get Episcopal High and Woodberry Forest boys. It seems to me

they got theirs from Grundy."

There you have it.

Bluebloods vs. bumpkins.

'Hoos 'n Hokies.

Just the kind of rivalry that feeds off inferiority complexes. As a land grant school, Tech had its share of those. From the start, the Hokies were fighting to shed their second-class status; they were hillbillies eager to gain acceptance and respect down in the lowlands. Those were things the Wahoos weren't about to give up, at least not without a fight and an insult or two. As time has shown, the Hokies were only happy to oblige.

It all began in 1895, when the games were rough affairs of pushing and punching. They looked more like rugby matches than modern football.

The ball was fat and round, suited for kicking or tucking under the arm, certainly not for passing. The field was long and wide. And rough. The players were small, but they exhibited a rakish toughness. They disdained padding as something for sissies. Rather than wear helmets, they grew their hair long to pad their heads when they smacked skulls.

The people who played "foot ball" were often considered goons and roughnecks. It seemed that someone was always writing a treatise defending the healthful aspects of the sport. Yet the games themselves were filled with bloodied noses, broken bones, and even an occasional fatality that scandalized Victorian sensibilities.

Society itself remained very much in the clutches of the nineteenth century. Most families still lived on farms, and even the typical city resident owned a cow. Commercial moving pictures had yet to be developed; the airplane and the automobile were just designers' dreams.

Like inhabitants of 1990s America, 1890s Americans approached the cusp of a new century with caution. The times were marked by international upheaval and economic uncertainty. The only surplus seemed to be poverty. Graft and crime were common. America's cities were young and small, but they were often dirty industrial centers that served as a breeding ground for domestic and labor disputes. Authorities frequently called on the militia to quell lynchings, riots, and strikes. There were ugly scenes of racial attacks on Americans of African, Italian, Chinese, and Japanese descent. Beneath all of these new conflicts festered the old one: the Civil War had ended just three decades earlier, and the wounds had not healed. The nation was fractured regionally.

Uncertainty bred a population that clung to nostalgic innocence. It was an age of bicycles and penny arcades and Sunday school picnics. Women wore corsets and full skirts; men sported straw hats, slightly tilted. Community brass bands were a favorite. "There'll Be A Hot Time In The Old Town Tonight" was the hit song. Yet all around were signs of change. There were newly invented wonders like the trolley car and the electric elevator. Ragtime music marked the country's quickening, nervous rhythm.

Industrialization created its share of problems, but with it also came an increase in leisure, something previously unheard of for many Americans. People hungered for more diversion. Sports, especially college football, provided cheap, quick alternatives. The game was evolving from English rugby with a series of rules changes. Walter Camp, the great Yale player and coach, prodded the sport along through the 1880s,

whittling the numbers of players on a side down to 11 from 15. Teams were allowed to alternate turns on offense, instead of playing a roving, kicking free-for-all. Slowly, the pattern of play became discernible to spectators.

By the time the sport arrived in the Old Dominion in the late 1880s, it had established only a little of the identity that eventually would make it popular among the American masses. Teams in those days before the forward pass had three downs to make five yards. Touchdowns counted four points, kicks after touchdowns were worth two, and a field goal counted five. The game was hardly one of finesse; despite football's movement away from rugby, it featured mostly a mass of players pushing and shoving each other.

Still, the sport had a captivating essence. During those years following the first American game between Princeton and Rutgers in 1869, football was something of an Ivy League fad. But the 1880s and 1890s saw its spread across the country. Colleges everywhere began adopting colors and organizing play. Almost immediately, school teams attracted the attention of alumni.

The University got out of the gate first, fielding a team in 1888. Because gridiron play was muddy, Virginia players decided not to wear the old Confederate gray and red uniforms they used for other sports. Instead, they held a meeting of the student athletic association to pick new colors. Allen Potts, one of the team's regulars, happened to wear a blue and orange scarf to the meeting that day. Another player grabbed it off Potts's neck and waved it in front of the crowd. "How will this do?" he asked.

Orange and blue it was, and the Wahoos were off and running. They won six games and lost three over their first two seasons. With that success, they rushed out and scheduled games with Princeton and Penn for 1890, a dreadful mistake. The Wahoos met the Quakers for the second game of the season in Washington and lost 72-0. Next up was powerhouse Princeton. A year earlier, a diminutive Virginian named Edgar Allan Poe had played end and served as team captain for the Tigers. He didn't compete in that 1890 game, but that didn't stop Virginia from getting buried alive, 115-0.

It was during this dreary 1890 campaign that Virginia fans supposedly came up with their trademark "Wah-Hoo-Wah" cheer. According to legend, the yell was probably borrowed from Dartmouth College; however, it's just as likely that "Wah-Hoo-Wah" was a wailing response to Virginia giving up 187 points in two games. Whatever the origin, the yell must have worked because the Wahoos closed the season with a four-game winning streak, including a venemous outburst of their own, a 136-0 win over Randolph-Macon.

By 1893, the Wahoos (referred to by *College Topics* in the early days of the program as "Old Dominion" and "Old Virginia") had established a reputation as a regional powerhouse. They finished 8-3, including a string of five shutouts over Trinity (Duke), Georgetown, Navy, Virginia Military, and North Carolina to end the season. Furthermore, the "Wah-Hoo-Wah" cheer got an extra workout when Natalie Floyd Otey was engaged to sing the Ballad "Where'er You Are, There Shall My Love Be" at the Levy Opera House in Charlottesville. Apparently Otey warbled the first three words of the refrain, prompting the student audience to sing along, corrupting the phrase to "Wah-Hoo-Wah" in the process.

That same season brought the appearance of the "Good Old Song." These spirited developments came just in time for Virginia's first game against Virginia Tech in 1895. The Hokies had started a football program of their own in 1892 and were eager to test their mettle against the Wahoos.

The Techsters had yet to develop their own little ditties—or much of a football squad. "It was not football," a critic explained in the 1892 *Bugle*, the Tech yearbook. "And yet we had some fun. . . . There was no idea of team play; whoever got the ball—by luck—ran with it. No one knew anything about interference, and though we had a system of signals, it was a question of luck how each play went."

Luck, it seems, was in abundance. The Hokies first opposition, a team from St. Albans—a local high school—arrived in three horsedrawn surries. On the sidelines, a hat was passed for admission. The team's second game, also against St. Albans, was cut short by a humongous argument over rules. In their second season, the Techsters lost both their games. But the 1894 campaign produced four wins and a narrow loss to VMI, leaving the Hokies thinking they were ready for Virginia.

The Wahoos had finished 8-2 in 1894, including victories over Rutgers and North Carolina and narrow losses to Princeton and Penn. They agreed to entertain the Techsters for the second game of the 1895 season, then made quick work of them, 38-0, on Lambeth Field.

It was an embarrassment for the Hokies, but they agreed to a rematch the next year. Tech's athletic identity emerged with that 1896 season. First, the school changed its name to Virginia Polytechnic Institute (VPI) and its athletic colors from grey and black to maroon and burnt orange. The school also adopted a mascot—a black man named Floyd "Hard Times" Meade.

With a new name and colors setting the tone, the school needed a fight song and sponsored a contest to get one. Cadet O.M. Stull won with:

> "Hoki, Hoki, Hoki Hy!
> Tech! Tech! VPI!
> Sola-Rex, Sola-Rah
> Polytech—Vir-gin-i-a!
> Rae, Ri, VPI!"

The "Hokies" were born. Years later, Stull admitted the word and cheer had no meaning. He just thought it sounded good. All this window dressing seemed to help the Techsters on the field—they finished 5-2-1—except when it came time for the trip to Charlottesville. Once again, the Wahoos ran away, this time 44-0.

"The visitors played a hard game and at times showed an unnecessary degree of roughness," noted *College Topics*, the University of Virginia student newspaper. "But we may offer in excuse their disappointment in finding themselves unable to hold the score down."

This defeat was enough to bring the rivalry a two-year rest. Yet when it resumed in 1899, the Hokies had no better luck, losing 28-0 in Charlottesville.

Finally, the 1900 game brought a slightly better fate. Although the Hokies were outgained 395 yards to 145, Tech at least scored on a Hunter Carpenter field goal before losing 17-5. "To the spectator, this game was very much marred by endless quarrels and interruptions," *College Topics* noted.

Immediately after the game, Tech's manager wired back to Blacksburg that the Hokies had been robbed. "We were sorry to learn that VPI considered herself

Hailed as "Two Great Tackles," Tech's C.P. Miles and Pete Wilson served five-year stints on the Hokie football team before more stringent rules regulating eligibility were mapped out. Miles coached the Hokies in their first victory over the Cavaliers in 1905.

badly treated in the game on Wednesday last," *College Topics* reported the next week. "The team gave an exhibition of puerile behavior at every decision of the umpire. . . ."

Each of the first four contests had been in Charlottesville with the officials arranged by the home team. "We're sorry, VPI, that you are always so down on your luck here," *College Topics* offered in an editorial, "and that no officials we've ever been able to furnish could see things enough your way to satisfy you." Perhaps it was the Hokies' constant complaining that finally forced the Wahoos to visit Blacksburg for the 1901 game.

"The day was perfect for a struggle," a newspaper reporter wrote of that October afternoon. "And as one looked out from the hills which hail the institution crown, in every direction could be seen clouds of dust following the carriages heralded by yellow flags and colors of orange and maroon."

Perhaps the Hokies should have proffered white flags. The Wahoos, on their way to an 8-2 season, prevailed yet again, 16-0. "When the whistle announced the end of the game, deep gloom enshrouded the whole cadet corps and campus," *College Topics* noted gleefully, "for her best chance of ever winning from Virginia was lost indisputably."

The next day, a Norfolk newspaper reported that "Virginia managed to win by her usual slugging."

The game returned to Charlottesville for the 1902 meeting, but Tech's hopes were high. The Hokies had beaten North Carolina State and Georgetown and tied Carolina in the weeks before the showdown. "Long before three o'clock the crowd began to assemble from all sides," *College Topics* reported. "Soon the grandstand was filled to overflowing and not just with Virginia rooters. There was quite a good sprinkling of VPI flags and colors, and in the early stages of the game some signs of life in the bearers thereof."

The game remained scoreless until Virginia's "Down Home" Council ran 23 yards for a score on a play disputed by the Hokies. They claimed the official should have blown the ball dead, to which *College Topics* surprisingly agreed the following week: "Our touchdown on Saturday was made through an oversight on the part of the referee—he forgot to call "Down Home" back, so we scored."

This close loss only served to increase the bitterness in Blacksburg. At the heart of the argument was Tech tackle C.P. "Sally" Miles, who was kicked out of the game. He would remain at Tech for years, first as coach, then as athletic director, and finally

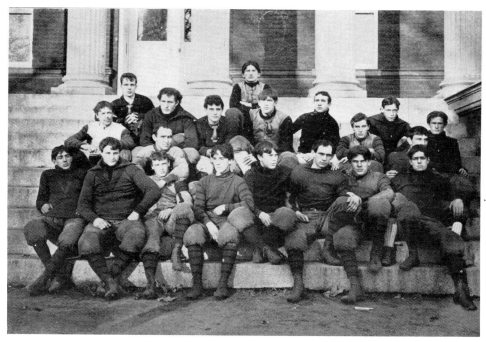

The 1895 Wahoos pose for a team picture.
They thrashed VPI 38-0 to begin this rivalry.

as president of the Southern Conference, all the time nurturing his dislike for the Wahoos.

In 1903, the site shifted to Richmond, but the outcome remained the same. Virginia won, 21-0, as "Down Home" Council led the rout with an 85-yard touchdown run. Better defense, it seemed, could be the only answer for the Techsters. To their credit, they again improved, but the outcome remained the same for 1904, a 5-0 Wahoo win in Richmond. "About 3,000 people saw the game," *College Topics* reported, "among whom were 300 cadets who came to Richmond on a special train. They did some good rooting, and the yells drowned the voices of the few Virginia rooters, whenever they attempted to make themselves heard."

Noise, however, wasn't going to win games. With each win, Tech's frustration and bitterness built, and the Wahoos' smugness deepened; the perfect recipe for hard feelings, the very seeds of hate.

Caius Hunter Carpenter was in every sense the quintessential Virginia Tech football player. He had the speed. The moves. The power. A well-timed straight arm. And, most important of all, he possessed an abiding desire to defeat the University of Virginia.

In fact, his obsession with beating the Wahoos was

so pronounced it carried him to the center of a great controversy between the schools that resulted in their refusing to play each other for eighteen years. One could even argue that the spirit of Hunter Carpenter swirls amid the low esteem in which the 'Hoos and Hokies hold one another today.

The reason for Hunter's mania was humiliation. In Tech's first eight games against Virginia, the Wahoos had mercilessly pounded the Hokies, outscoring them by a grand total of 170 to 5.

Carpenter received his diploma in 1903, after playing what amounted to five seasons at Tech without coming close to beating Virginia. With that stigma burning in the back of his brain, he decided to pursue graduate studies at the University of North Carolina, mainly because the Tar Heels had a strong team and a good chance of whipping the Wahoos. Carpenter wanted a win, even if he had to change uniforms to get it.

The loosely organized college athletic associations had no firm eligibility rules in that era, a situation that allowed Carpenter to stretch out his playing days to seven full seasons. He stayed out of the lineup when Carolina played VPI that fall, but for the Virginia game he was more than ready.

The 1904 contest between Carolina and Virginia was played at Richmond's Broad Street Park, where

15,000 fans crammed the sidelines to watch Carpenter take on the Cavaliers. The eight police officers on duty that day were easily outmanned, and twice the crowd pushed onto the field, delaying the game for more than a half hour.

Carolina scored three times, including a 15-yard touchdown run by Carpenter. But Virginia kept pace and won, 12-11, in the closing seconds, when a Carolina player inadvertently tipped the Wahoos' final extra point try between the goal posts for a score.

The loss left Carpenter despondent. Turning down an offer to be captain of Carolina's 1905 team, he decided to return to Tech as a graduate student to play one more year for the Hokies.

It was Tech's first 10-game schedule, and the players responded with a banner offensive season, racking up 305 points in the days when a touchdown counted only five points (a scoring record that even modern teams have struggled to better).

The Hokies ripped through five straight victories, including an 86-0 defeat of Roanoke College, during which Carpenter was said to average better than 20 yards per carry. Tech tried using all of its subs to hold down the score, but the touchdowns kept coming. Finally both sides agreed to call the game after 25 minutes of play, meaning that Tech scored about 3.44 points per minute. Next came an upset of national powerhouse Army at West Point, followed by a 35-6 win over North Carolina.

The force in these wins was Carpenter, whose reputation as a large, swift, multitalented back had built with each succeeding season. With Carpenter's rise to regional notoriety, the Hokies drew larger and larger crowds. Suddenly, VPI games became a social event. Tech men cheered the team on, and their dates wore orange and maroon ribbons. "See Carpenter Play Football," announced the handbills promoting Tech's games. With each VPI win, the interest grew.

The 1905 version of the Wahoos wasn't bad, either. They had won four games and lost one, to the powerful Carlisle Indians. But the usual trouble struck in the weeks before the Tech game. Three Wahoos went down with broken collarbones. The rash of injuries meant that the team was receptive when Pops Lanigan, a new coach, appeared on campus and introduced them to a new "old" game, Association Football, or soccer. Leading up to the meeting with VPI, the Virginia

football team spent its afternoons playing soccer, a good way to stay in shape yet avoid injuries, coach William Cole figured.

All the while, the state's newspapers focused on Carpenter's play, especially the week before the Tech-UVa meeting, when the big back led the Hokies to an unprecedented win at Army. These reports served to unsettle the Wahoos, according to *College Topics*. "Knowing what a heavy body of men compose the Blacksburg contingent and taking into account their splendid victory over West Point, it is not strange that the student body here felt uneasiness as to the probable outcome of the game Saturday. . . ."

To bolster their manpower, the Wahoos were struck by the idea of bringing in a well-known player who had recently flunked out of Columbia. The students held a rally in support of this idea, but the faculty voted to admit the athlete as a student but not to allow him to play football. To do otherwise, one faculty member noted, would leave the University open to charges of using a "ringer."

Meanwhile, there was trouble of a similar sort brewing for Tech. Virginia players had been grousing that Carpenter and four or five of his teammates were actually professionals, athletes playing for room and board and sometimes pay. The idea of an athletic scholarship was scandalous to Victorian sensibilities. To clarify this matter, the Virginia athletic managers had written to Blacksburg earlier in the season requesting that the Tech players sign affadavits that they were all eligible as amateurs; the Hokies complied.

The issue, however, resurfaced in the week before the game. *College Topics* claimed that Virginia's athletic management had "absolute evidence" that Carpenter was playing for money. The Wahoos would not play, the newspaper said, unless Carpenter "would stand trial before a jury of unprejudiced men."

The student newspaper also implied that there was similar evidence against five other Tech players, but added that "Virginia admitted that they had no sufficient proof to bar them from the game, but if that proof they were looking for arrived before the game on Saturday, that those men could not play. . . ."

Sally Miles, now the coach at Tech, scoffed at these propositions, including a "trial" for Carpenter.

The debate and the university's decision not to allow the transfer student from Columbia to play

Hard Times

Floyd "Hard Times" Meade, Tech's first mascot, was a gifted one-man band who dressed as a clown and entertained the crowds in Blacksburg, which by 1896 had begun to reach 400 or so for big games. Though he remained a part of the Tech football scene for many years, Meade eventually dropped his clown act and spent months training what he called "the largest turkey in Montgomery County." He then hitched the bird to a small cart and rode around the field before games to entertain the fans. It was an act that would further entrench the growing VPI nickname of "Fighting Gobblers." And it became a Tech tradition for Meade to train a turkey each fall to pull his cart around the field for the Thanksgiving Day game. When his toil was over, the bird would then meet an appointment with the axe, the oven, and the banquet table, certainly circumstances that would require a gobbler to fight.

Tech's 1895 team, with captain Lewis "Nig" Ingles holding the ball, was the first to play against Virginia.

caused such an uproar on Virginia's campus that university president Edwin A. Alderman agreed to a meeting to calm the Virginia student body. He had little luck.

That next afternoon, the manager of the student-run athletic association called for a mass meeting of the student body in Madison Hall to vote on whether the Wahoos should agree to play against Carpenter. According to the *Richmond Times Dispatch*, the athletic manager then read the following telegram from the president and secretary of the school's Norfolk alumni association:

"Note protest and sever future relations. Then play Blacksburg with Carpenter, though rank professional-

plans to play. On Thursday, two days before the game, Virginia athletic officials sent word that the contest was off and the guarantee of Tech's expense money was revoked. Not to be denied, Carpenter and the team went to Tech's student body and raised the money for the trip to Charlottesville. With their own expense money, the Techsters informed Virginia they were coming anyway.

"We left Blacksburg on Friday and went to Lynchburg by train," Tech coach C.P. "Sally" Miles recalled 50 years later. "We took our meals in bags and ate in our rooms so there would be no trouble. But we still didn't know if the game would be played."

That Saturday morning, a *Norfolk Virginian Pilot*

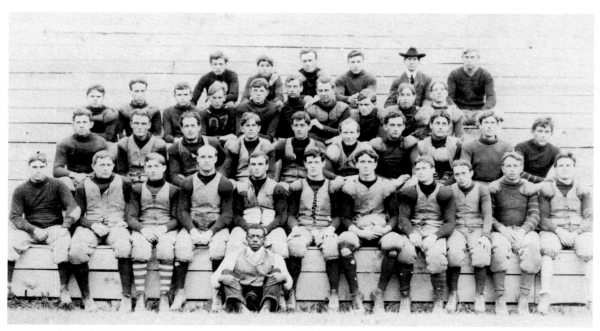

The 1905 Tech team was the first to defeat UVa, and was eventually named "Champions of the South." (Photo VT Special Collections)

ism proved. We see nothing else will satisfy alumni and State. Besides, we believe Carpenter only one of many professionals in Blacksburg, and we think you will win anyway."

The student manager then put to vote the notion that Virginia would play the game "and that thereafter athletic relations should be severed between the two institutions."

"The crowd rose practically as one man" in voting to sever, the *Times Dispatch* reported.

The Hokies, meanwhile, were pushing ahead with

reporter showed up at the Hokies hotel and asked Carpenter, "Well, do you expect to play?"

"Certainly I expect to play," the Tech star replied.

As expected, the widely publicized debate brought greater interest in the game. "All day the streets of Charlottesville were filled with visiting alumni and members of the VPI cadets corps," *College Topics* reported. "The old boys drove up and down the streets singing the 'Good Old Song' and yelling the varsity yells as they did in the old days. An excursion from Norfolk brought up 22 of the Norfolk alumni, and the morning trains from Richmond and Staunton swelled the lists.

"At one o'clock the crowds commenced to sweep by the University post office and at two o'clock there was a far larger crowd assembled on Lambeth field than has ever collected there heretofore. Virginia rooters held the bleachers and 'Happy' Chandler was right in front ready to call for a yell as soon as the varsity should appear. Gaily and peculiarly dressed, the Lambda Pi Nu, Sigma Nu, and Phi Ro Sigma goats did stunts to amuse the crowd till time for kick off."

At 2:16, the Hokies appeared on the field, and a few minutes later the Wahoos came out to toss the ball around. Then the teams' two captains met at midfield to debate the rules, especially the length of the game. Once that was settled, Wahoo captain M.T. Cooke turned to call his teammates out on the field, but the student-led athletic association turned them back.

Virginia officials then presented another affadavit for Carpenter and his teammates to sign, which led to an animated discussion on the Tech sideline. The Hokies argued that they had made all the assurances necessary, while the Wahoos repeated their allegations that certain players had been given tuition in return for playing.

The standoff persisted until the 3:00 P.M. starting time neared and the Wahoos relented and took the field. "The affadavit which the gentlemen from VPI had been requested to sign was read to the bleachers," *College Topics* reported, "and the teams lined up to kick off."

It was the moment Carpenter had waited for, and he met it with fire. He broke the Wahoos' hopes with a good touchdown run, used his kicking to keep Virginia near its own goal, and impressed the newspapermen on the sidelines with his vicious tackling. As was typical of early football, the game was marked by much punching and foul language. Carpenter repeatedly warned one Virginia player to quit hitting him.

Tech had built an 11-0 lead, when late in the game Carpenter broke loose on a long run. The Wahoo who had slugged Carpenter several times earlier grabbed the Tech back by the neck and took another swing. Carpenter stopped, decked his opponent, tossed the ball into the crowd and left the field one step ahead of the official's ejection whistle.

Virginia again went on the offensive, yet even without Carpenter the fired-up Tech defense held. When it became apparent Virginia couldn't advance, the game was called. "They kept the time," Sally Miles

recalled, "and we played until it was nearly dark. I learned after the game that the second half had lasted about sixty-five minutes."

The game was over, but the dispute had only begun. "Virginia Was Fairly Beaten," the *Richmond Times Dispatch* declared in its headline the next day.

Citing the editorial attacks on his character, Carpenter and his father took steps to file a libel suit against *College Topics*. After repeated efforts, they extracted an apology from the newspaper's editor and dropped the matter.

Relations between the two schools worsened, however, and they did not play again until the 1923 season after time had blurred their dispute. As late as 1938, Carpenter was still protesting his amateur status. "I never received help, financial or otherwise, for playing football," he told his nephew, Deverton Carpenter, who was a Richmond newspaper reporter. "My father [a well-to-do Clifton Forge businessman] paid all my college expenses, and if I had received any help, he would have made me quit playing football or withdraw from the team the moment he heard of it. Those charges were absolutely untrue."

The fact that Carpenter played seven years of college ball should be considered in the context that he never played in high school. He entered Tech in the fall of 1898 at age 15 weighing 128 pounds and almost immediately became fascinated with the game. He answered the call for recruits, only to have the coach say he was too small. But he had decided football was a man's game and figured he would hang around practice for the opportunity to play. He put cleats on a pair of old shoes, donned a sweater and a pair of old football pants, and waited patiently behind the scrub team as it scrimmaged the varsity.

When a varsity player broke through the line headed for a touchdown, Carpenter nailed him with a surprise tackle. "Listen you," Carpenter recalled the irate player saying as he got up, "if you keep this up, I'll grind your face in the dirt, and your own mother won't be able to recognize you."

The effort earned him a spot as a scrub but wasn't enough to get him into a game. The second year was only a little better. He weighed 150 pounds, and the coach gave him a uniform. But he still didn't play much. Then in 1900, he became the team's starting right halfback. There was only one problem. His father, J.C. Hunter Carpenter, had forbidden him to play football, so Hunter competed under the name of Walter Brown. It didn't take long for a newspaper reporter to discover his real name.

Still, his cover wasn't blown until the 1900 VMI matchup in Norfolk, where he played an exceptional game, leading the Hokies to a 50-5 smashing of the Keydets. Carpenter's father, who had been brought there by a friend, watched incredulously from the bleachers. Afterward, young Carpenter was aglow with victory when he unexpectedly encountered his old man in the lobby of the Monticello Hotel. The senior was so overcome by his son's performance that he relented.

"If you want to play football, go ahead," his father said. "But if you continue, I want you to do your best. Anything worth doing is worth doing well."

By 1901, he weighed 197 pounds and was clocked in the 100-yard dash at 10.4 seconds. Over the next four seasons, he became "The Great Carpenter," a regional legend across Virginia and Carolina. "Get Carpenter" became the yell for opposing teams, and he answered with a flair that would be remembered for decades after his playing career had ended.

Yet, at the time he played, Carpenter wasn't well-known outside of the region. Southern football didn't attract much notice in those days. The northern teams, especially the Ivy League schools, were the power-houses. Walter Camp, the legendary Yale player and coach who picked the All-America teams, didn't include southern players. Despite Hunter Carpenter's big reputation in the South, he was overlooked by Camp.

The oversight, however, would be remedied a half century later, in part because Carpenter's performance against Army that November of 1905 burned an

Tech's Hunter Carpenter is lined up behind center in this photo taken around the turn of the century.

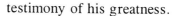

Left: **The man who helped start it all — Hunter Carpenter.**

testimony of his greatness.

"We had not heard of Hunter Carpenter," recalled Colonel Charles C. Mettler, a tackle and captain of Army's 1905 squad. "Before we were aware of Hunter Carpenter, VPI had scored a touchdown. We tried a bit harder with some substitutions, and VPI scored again.

"Hunter Carpenter played all over the field, ran the team expertly, diagnosed our plays, blocked our runners, interfered with our kicks, charged through our line with great speed and power, and held us for downs under the old rules. We were surprised, confused, and defeated by this one dynamic leader of a small team. I have never forgotten him, nor have my classmates allowed me to do so, for over 50 years."

Douglas McKay, a member of South Carolina's 1905 team, wrote that "Carpenter was a back in the caliber of Jim Thorpe, Red Grange, and others of that caliber." Former Keydets from VMI, Tar Heels

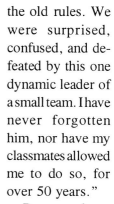

indelible impression into the minds of his opponents. By ripping off long runs, booming great punts, and playing fearsome defense, he had led Tech to a 16-6 upset of the Cadets.

In 1955, Tech athletic director emeritus Sally Miles led a drive to have Carpenter named posthumously to the College Football Hall of Fame. Several players from opposing teams stepped forward to offer

from Carolina, even several Wahoos, offered similar endorsements to the Hall of Fame. Based on that evidence, Carpenter was elected in 1956.

His favorite teammate was Charles E. "Cub" Bear, a blocking back who often led the way for Carpenter's long runs. In later years, Carpenter recalled how sometimes he would latch on to Cub Bear's jersey and hitch a ride through the opposition.

"I have seen lots of games, and nearly all of the bowl games since [his playing days]," Bear wrote in 1955, "and I have yet to see a man who could play football like Hunter Carpenter."

Especially when it came to lining up against the Wahoos.

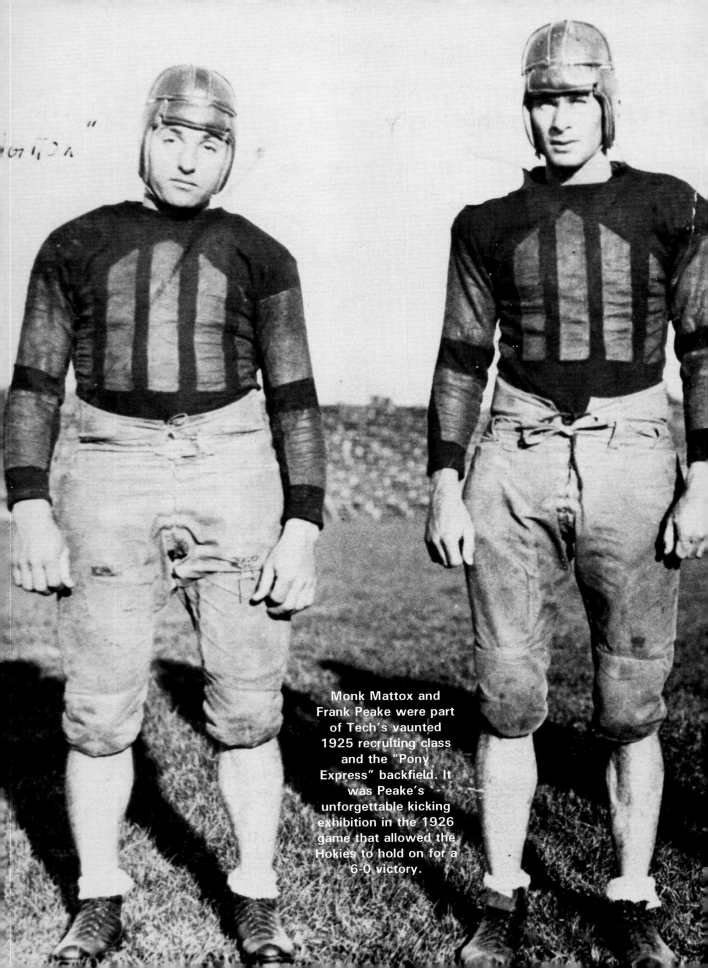

Monk Mattox and Frank Peake were part of Tech's vaunted 1925 recruiting class and the "Pony Express" backfield. It was Peake's unforgettable kicking exhibition in the 1926 game that allowed the Hokies to hold on for a 6-0 victory.

HECKLED BY FATE

"For men of two institutions of higher learning, men who have never seen each other, to harbor animosity toward each other, is hard to conceive. Is Virginia too good for VPI? Why? Are VPI men envious of Virginia men? Why?"

—*Virginia Tech*, student newspaper
November 1931

Sadly, Virginia and Virginia Tech wasted some of their best seasons squabbling over the Hunter Carpenter fiasco. Between 1906 and 1922, both schools fielded teams consistently among the best in southern college football. Regardless, each stubbornly persisted in pretending the other didn't exist.

"There was too much feeling between the two teams," Mel Jeffries, a 1927 Tech graduate and the school's sports publicist for many years, explained in a 1984 interview. "Virginia was sort of flaunting its attitude of purity in athletics and kind of pointing its finger at Virginia Tech. And

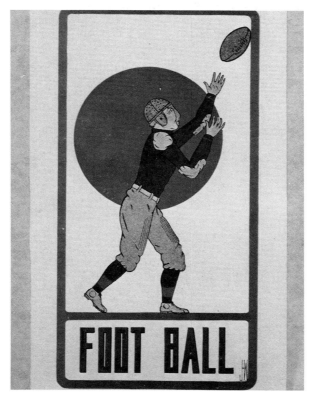

The program cover for a Tech football game in the mid-1920's.

Tech was equally critical of Virginia's way of handling athletics."

Over the 17-year period, both schools won 67 percent of their games. The Hokies posted a 96-41-8 record while the Wahoos were 90-36-9. Tech's program featured wins over Maryland, Tennessee, Clemson, North Carolina, North Carolina State, Mississippi, West Virginia, and Wake Forest, while the Wahoos whipped Yale, Vanderbilt, Georgia, South Carolina, Navy, North Carolina, and North Carolina State.

Clearly, the two schools were the best in the state of Virginia at the time, and their

Tech prepares to receive a kick at new Miles Field circa 1907.

obstinance resulted in numerous missed opportunities for classic showdowns. For instance:

- 1907, Tech was 7-2 and Virginia 6-3-1
- 1908, Virginia was 7-0-1 and Tech was 5-4 with narrow losses to Princeton, Navy, and North Carolina State
- 1909, the Hokies were 6-1 and the Wahoos were 7-1 (and both claimed the "Championship of the South")
- 1910, both were 6-2
- 1911, Virginia was 8-2 and the Hokies were 6-1-2
- 1913, the Wahoos were 7-1 and the Hokies 7-1-1
- 1914 and 1915, Eugene Mayer led the Wahoos to a 16-2 record
- 1916-1918, the Hokies were 20-4-1, including an eleven- game winning streak leading into the 1919 season.

One reason the cold relations persisted was that students and alumni ran the football program at Virginia for much of the period. Despite efforts to change this, each successful season only reinforced the old system. "Hereafter, no one need say a word against the Alumni Coaching System," the university's *Alumni News* wrote during the 1915 season, "unless he wishes to stir up the hornets. It has brought results."

Tech, on the other hand, had formed an athletic association in 1908, begun selling season tickets, and hired the University of Georgia's bright young coach, Branch Bocock, who ran the program from 1909 to 1915, though he spent the 1911 season as North Carolina's coach. Still, Bocock hardly qualified as a big-time "professional" coach because he also had teaching duties at the school.

The game itself took on a new face during the early decades of the new century. When President Theodore Roosevelt called for changes in football after the 1905 season, college officials decided that violence could be reduced if each team was allowed four downs to gain ten yards, instead of three to get five, which had resulted in fierce battles on the line of scrimmage.

Legalizing the forward pass further opened the game, and the use of padding and leather headgear

"Wop" Sutton

Above left: Henry "Puss" Redd, a noted English scholar, was anything but gentlemanly toward Virginia when he presided over the Hokies' program as head coach. Redd was 6-1-2 against the Cavs during his tenure with the Hokies from 1932-40.

Above right: Stout tackle Bill Grinus captained the 1932 Tech team that compiled a record of 8-1, including a 13-0 shutout of Virginia.

Left: In 1923, Wop Sutton scored the only touchdown to give Tech a 6-3 victory over UVa in the first game played between the two schools since 1905.

Tex Tilson captained the 1921 Hokie squad that went 7-3.

the sport at the University. But the Wahoos marched on with their program, turning Lambeth Field into Lambeth Stadium in 1913 with a $35,000 construction project that created 8,000 seats.

Virginia did not field a team for two seasons, 1917-1918, during World War I; however, the debate over alumni coaching resurfaced shortly after the Armistice. The school had grown to a student body of 2,000. Surprisingly, the students voted to hire a professional coach in December of 1919. Dr. Rice Warren was the first hire; he lasted two mediocre seasons and was followed by Thomas Campbell for the 1922 campaign.

The college game had continued to change dramatically, with schools across the South hiring coaches and making plans to grant athletic scholarships. One sign of this change was the formation of the Southern Intercollegiate Conference in 1920, which would become the Southern Conference in 1923, a twenty-eight-team league that would include the universities of Georgia, Alabama, South Carolina, North Carolina, and Tennessee, as well as numerous other major colleges.

Tech, meanwhile, posted a 15-4-1 record in 1921-1922 with Ben Cubbage, a chemistry professor, serving as coach. This crystallized the Wahoos' need to find the right man to lead their program.

Their choice, as it turned out, was a classic. Earle "Greasy" Neale, who had earned his nickname with

became a standard. Both Tech and Virginia found success in this new format, which emphasized speed and execution over brute strength.

Yet those changes didn't prevent the tragedy of fatal injuries to Virginia player Archer Christian during a 1909 game at Georgetown, bringing cries to eliminate

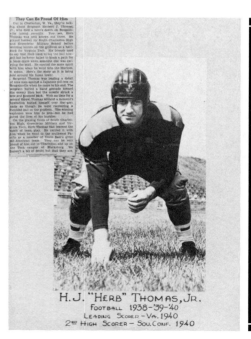

H. J. "HERB" THOMAS, JR.
FOOTBALL 1938-'39-'40
LEADING SCORER - VA. 1940
2ND HIGH SCORER - SOU.CONF. 1940

Left: Herb Thomas enjoyed a stellar career with the Hokies; in his last game against the UVa, the Hokies prevailed 6-0.

Right: George Smith, who captained the Hokies in 1934.

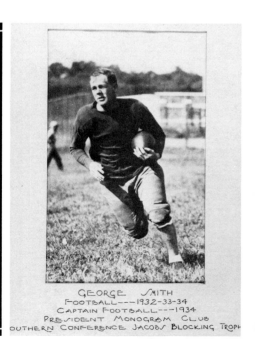

GEORGE SMITH
FOOTBALL---1932-33-34
CAPTAIN FOOTBALL---1934
PRESIDENT MONOGRAM CLUB
SOUTHERN CONFERENCE JACOBS BLOCKING TROPH

his penchant for trick plays, was one of the hottest coaches in the country in 1923, having just directed little Washington and Jefferson College to an undefeated season and a scoreless tie in the 1922 Rose Bowl with the University of California, a national powerhouse.

A psychological master, Neale had employed a tactic to disconcert Cal's great running back, Brick Muller. When Muller checked into the muddy game for his first offensive set, Neale instructed each of his players to walk up and wipe their hands on Muller's clean uniform and say, "So this is

The 1908 Tech team finished with a record of 5-4.

Tech's coaches
William C. Younger and Tex Tilson.

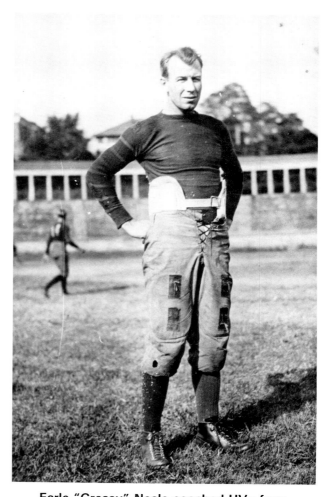

Earle "Greasy" Neale coached UVa from 1923-28 and guided the Cavs to a record of 28-22-5. Neale played a key role in the resumption of the series in 1923. His teams split six games with the Hokies.

the great Brick Muller."

After Virginia, Neale would coach at West Virginia and Yale, where he was credited with developing the five-man defensive front, and from there would move on to coach the National Football League's Philadelphia Eagles to two championships.

In 1923, Neale had enough of a reputation to quiet the squawking of the powerful Virginia alumni groups over the hiring of an outsider. With a new coach, the team needed a new image, and that season *College Topics* sponsored a contest to choose an official fight song. "The Cavalier Song," written by Lawrence Haywood Lee, Jr., class of 1924, won the competition. The song failed to become part of the team's tradition, but the use of the nickname "Cavaliers" stuck, and soon the name was interchangeable with Wahoos.

Neale also realized the importance of reviving the series with Virginia Tech and agreed to the resumption of the game in 1923. "The attitudes on both sides had softened a bit, and the public wanted it," Mel Jeffries said of the schools' decision to renew the rivalry.

College Topics reported that several attempts had been made over the years to patch up differences

The 1909 Virginia Tech team finished 7-1 and called itself the "The Champions of the South." Virginia also finished the season 7-1 and proclaimed itself champion, but the temporary halt of the series cost fans the opportunity to see the two teams compete.

between the schools, but ill feelings had remained strong. No one could seem to remember exactly what caused the original disagreement, the student newspaper said. "Whatever the trouble, the games stopped, and efforts to arrange another contest were of no avail."

News of the renewed rivalry brought 3,000 advance ticket sales for the November 17 game and speculation that the crowd could exceed 10,000, *College Topics*

The 1936 Tech team defeated UVa 7-6 with VPI's only score coming on a tipped pass that went for a touchdown.

recent years, and they were led by All-Southern back Wop Sutton. Still, most figured the game would be close because Neale had a reputation for excellent defensive teams.

The Hokies fumbled in the first quarter, giving Virginia a first and goal at the four. But two running plays netted only a yard, and on third down, Wahoo back Sam Maphis was thrown for an 11-yard loss while attempting to pass. On fourth down, the center snapped the ball over Maphis' head, and Tech took over on the 35-yard line. Later in the period, Virginia quarterback G.B. Arnold punched up a 45-yard drop kick that hit one side of the goal post and fell through for a 3-0 Wahoo lead.

In the second quarter, Tech's Don Rutherford missed three drop kicks, then missed two more in the third and fourth periods. Then late in the game, the Hokies drove to Virginia's 25-yard line. Wop Sutton dropped back to pass, but was unable to find a receiver and ran the ball to the eight. Two plays later, he scored. The conversion failed, but the Hokies led 6-3.

Neale then called on backup quarterback Henry Foster, who produced what must have been the original

Above: Virginia Tech coach Ben Cubbage helped guide the Hokies to a 6-3 win over Virginia in 1923, but it would be his only victory in the series.

Right: A capacity crowd at Lambeth Field watched the resumption of the series in 1923.

reported. "Crowds of football enthusiasts larger than ever before seen on Lambeth Field are pouring in, and the seating capacity of the stadium and bleachers will be taxed to the utmost."

Most prognosticators seemed to favor the Hokies because they had clearly enjoyed more success in

two-minute drill. Foster hit passes for 27, 10, and 20 yards to move the Wahoos into scoring position. The sub quarterback then completed another 10-yard play, but was injured and had to leave the game. The Virginia offense stalled with a missed drop kick, and the Hokies held on to win their second game in the series.

Afterward, both sides agreed that the game was marked by an unusual degree of sportsmanship.

For 1924, the teams agreed to meet in Blacksburg at Miles Field. And again the game was marked by intense defense and missed drop kicks. In the opening minutes, Virginia's W.H. Ahner picked up a loose ball and ran 40-yards for a score. "The first play after the kickoff, Jack Moss took the ball and bucked into the line," recalled longtime Hokie Mac McEver. "His foot hit the pitcher's mound at old Miles Field, and he stumbled and fumbled. Ahner, the Virginia end, picked up the ball and ran for a touchdown, and that was the end of the scoring. It was a muddy day."

Neale's defense was tough even on dry ground, and the score gave Virginia a 6-0 win. The shortage of offense was typical for Cubbage's late Tech teams. Over the 1924 and 1925 seasons, the Hokies played five scoreless ties.

Neale, meanwhile, produced his best Virginia team in 1925 with a 7-1-1 record. Against Tech at Lambeth Field, the Wahoos showed enough passing game for a 10-0 win. The Hokies threatened to score only once, but the Wahoos blocked Tech's drop kick. Only 6,000 had seen the game, an indication that few Hokie fans attended. "Cubbage's team dropped off a bit in 1925 [to 5-3-2], and the alumni weren't satisfied with him," McEver recalled.

Now that Virginia had a "name" coach, the Hokies wanted one, too. So they hired Andy Gustafson, who had played at the University of Pittsburgh under Pop Warner and Jock Sutherland. As an assis-

Legendary Virginia coach Art Guepe, then a backfield coach, gives instructions to 1939 team captain Jim Gillette.

tant, Gustafson brought in Zonar Wissinger, who had been an All-American at Pitt in 1924. They installed a double wing offense behind an unbalanced line.

Just as important, however, was the fact that Tech had begun giving athletic scholarships in 1925, and its first recruiting class included the "Pony Express" backfield led by a gliding, graceful runner named Frank Woodfin Peake. McEver, Tommy Tomko, Scotty McArthur, and Monk Mattox rounded out the Pony Express, which gained a quick reputation by trouncing all their freshman team opposition.

In one quick recruiting class, the Hokies had produced an offensive threat. But Gustafson was also defense-minded. Tech used that combination to push past the Wahoos 6-0 in 1926 in a game that marked the dedication of the new Miles Stadium in Blacksburg. Mostly, the crowd got to see a kicking exhibition by Tech's Peake that kept the Wahoos frustrated all day.

"Finding it impossible to penetrate the Gobblers' line, Virginia was forced to resort to the passing game," *College Topics* reported, "and twice had the ball deep in enemy terrain only to lose it."

Like the 1926 contest, the 1927 game featured another punting duel between Peake and Virginia's talented John Sloan, with Peake's spirals threatening to push the Wahoos right off their home field. On the first series, the Hokies drove to the Virginia three-yard line, but the Wahoos held. They drove out, only to be shoved back down to their five in the second quarter by another Peake punt. But from there, Sloan took over for Virginia.

Tech back Duncan Holsclaw.

In what has to be the guttiest play in the history of the rivalry, the Virginia back faked a punt from his own five and ran 45 yards for a first down. Then he passed for 10 and followed up with a 26-yard chug around left end. After a four-yard dive play, Sloan took a lateral and scored from the 10. The 7-0 advantage was all Virginia would need. Five times the Hokies drove inside the Virginia 20, yet they couldn't score.

The Wahoos, however, only finished the season 5-4, and when a flurry of injuries sank them to 2-6-1 in 1928, it was time for the colorful Neale to depart. The Hokies, meanwhile, pranced off behind Peake and the Pony Express to Gustafson's best season. With wins over Maryland and Carolina and a single loss to nationally ranked Colgate, they entertained a demoralized Virginia team for Homecoming in Blacksburg.

The week of the game, the Virginia student newspaper, *College Topics*, launched a campaign to have Tech dropped from the schedule. "It has been a question here for several years as to the desirability of playing VPI," the editors concluded, adding that the Wahoos would be better off scheduling Tulane or another school that could bring "more value."

The article immediately became bulletin board material for the Hokies. "Possibly these statements have accounted for more than one Gobbler touchdown," *Virginia Tech*, the Hokie student newspaper commented wryly.

The editorials provided just the inspiration to make the Hokies play hurt. Peake had been injured against Maryland, a week before the 1928 showdown, and was laid up in the Tech infirmary for five days. Although he had strict instructions not to play, the star back talked the college doctor into allowing him to attend the game. Once in the locker room, Peake sold Gustafson on the idea of suiting up just so he could sit on the bench with the team.

A wet snow fell that Saturday, November 10, leaving the crowd of 7,000 chilled and quiet. Very quickly the game took on the familiar feel of previous seasons. Virginia drove deep into Tech territory four times but couldn't score. Halfback Phil Spear scored a second-quarter touchdown for the Hokies. Then, just before half, Tech drove deep again only to see the drive stalled on the Virginia 11. At that point, Peake began begging Gustafson to let him run it.

The program for Tech's 31-13 victory in 1930.

The 1935 game ended in a scoreless tie

A product of the UVa sports information office.

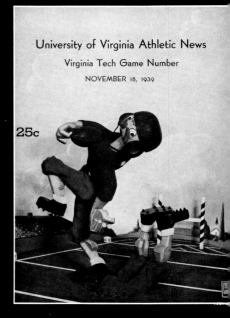

"Peake's hurt resembled that of Babe Ruth, who, although supposed to be physically incapacitated, managed to do fairly well in the recent World Series against the St. Louis Cardinals," *College Topics* observed.

Gustafson relented, and in three quick plays Peake rushed to a first down, and then the touchdown.

The scenario repeated itself in the third quarter

Actually, Abell's 1929 team started 4-1-1, with a win over South Carolina and a tie against Maryland. Although injuries had eliminated Sloan, now a senior, and veteran tackle Larry Whalen, the Wahoos opened strong against Tech at Lambeth Field. They intercepted a pass and scored quickly in the first period, then came right back with a sustained drive to take a 12-0 lead.

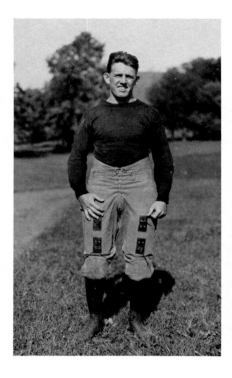

Far left: Tech's Dick Esleeck was a member of the All-South Atlantic team in 1924.

Left: Tech's Henry Crisp.

Bottom: Frank Peake and Scotty MacArthur formed the core of the Hokies' vaunted Pony Express backfield.

Opposite: The cover of the 1928 game program.

when Peake asked Gustafson to allow him to return a punt. "They won't touch me," the back allegedly promised. "He caught a punt from Sloan on his own 30-yard line and twisted and side-stepped his way through the entire Virginia team for a 70-yard run and a touchdown," *College Topics* reported. "Peake's brilliant run was easily the prettiest piece of individual work seen during the game. . . ."

"See," Peake reportedly told Gustafson as he came back to the bench, "I told you they wouldn't touch me."

Tech closed out the game 20-0, and the Pony Express ran to their best season, a 7-2 finish.

To replace Neale, Virginia hired Earl Abell out of Colgate, but it didn't work out. "He simply wasn't able," quipped longtime Wahoo fan Dr. John Risher.

Official Souvenir Program

PRESIDENT BURRUSS
V.P.I.

PRESIDENT ALDERMAN
Virginia

V.P.I.

VA.

CAPT. "HOCK" BAILEY
V.P.I.

CAPT. BILL LUKE
Virginia

Home-Coming Game

MILES FIELD, NOVEMBER 10, 1928
BLACKSBURG, VIRGINIA

The Hokies answered to make it 12-7 in the opening series of the second period. Sloan then came off the bench to thrill the Virginia crowd with a 40-yard run that put the Wahoos in scoring position again. The game, however, hinged on the next few plays as Virginia threw an interception and watched Tech turn that into a 13-12 lead on McEver's touchdown run. The Wahoos got the ball back and promptly threw another interception that led to another quick Tech score and a 19-12 Hokie lead.

Dedication of Miles Stadium in 1926.

The two teams smashed back and forth throughout the third period, but Hokie back Phil Spear settled the issue in the fourth quarter with two touchdowns (giving him four on the afternoon) to drive Tech to its biggest win, 32-12. The loss seemed to mark the downturn for Abell. The Wahoos finished the season by tying Washington and Lee and losing big to North Carolina.

Tech's Gustafson departed in the wake of a 5-4 season, to be replaced by Orville "Slippery" Neale, an interim coach from Western Maryland. His first team finished 5-3-1. The 1930 season wasn't any better for Virginia, with big losses to Duke, Penn, Maryland, and Carolina. The Tech game produced the Wahoos' third straight loss to the Hokies-another big one, 34-13.

In the days before the game, *College Topics* had renewed its campaign to drop Tech from the schedule. "Our reason for dropping VPI is simply a lack of interest in the game," the editors noted. "We have no hard feelings against the Blacksburg institution—and no more than a respectful fear of their football team; but we believe that football contests without some element of interest too easily become considered only

Virginia runs a dive play against the Hokies in 1927 at Lambeth Field.

slightly more than drudgery."

The Wahoos finished 4-6 in 1930, and Abell was replaced by Fred Dawson, a Princeton man whose teams would compile an 8-17-4 record over the next three seasons. Tech itself wasn't much better in 1931, running up a 3-4-2 record. With *College Topics* again calling for an end to the series, the two teams met in Charlottesville in brand new Scott Stadium, which had opened in October. Their efforts produced a scoreless tie. Rischer recalled that one newspaper reporter quipped that Tech and Virginia "had played for the booby prize of the South and tied!"

Virginia had actually come close to scoring, but the officials called back a Wahoo touchdown after ruling that Virginia back William Thomas had stepped out on the three-yard line. Even a first and goal at the three couldn't get Virginia a score, and the finish reflected the two programs' futility. In a headline, *College Topics* noted that the Wahoos seemed "Heckled by Fate."

After the game, the Virginia Tech student newspaper published an editorial lamenting that the "persistence of the feeling between the schools . . . has become an inheritance, passed on to incoming students. . . .

"It further will be realized that the attitude is ridiculous."

The Tech editorial was reprinted without comment in *College Topics*.

Actually, the problem at both schools seemed to be a lack of interest in athletics. Mac McEver noted that Tech's 1932 freshman class contained no scholarship athletes. In Charlottesville and Blacksburg, the mood pointed toward decline, and athletic officials at both schools seemed not to care.

"We just weren't keeping up with the times," recalled McEver, who had graduated and taken a job as a Tech assistant coach at the time. "Everybody else had organizations going. They were getting money from alumni and going commercial. They were getting scholarships and going out and finding players. Deans were putting in courses that athletes could take. In Virginia, we were just behind the times."

Alabama, Georgia, Tennessee, Vanderbilt, and numerous other schools wanted to become more serious about sports. They wanted to begin radio broadcasts of their games and to initiate fundraising campaigns among their alumni. But Tech Athletic Director Sally Miles, as president of the Southern Conference, fought these changes. The object of athletics, he said in one speech, was not so much to win "but to fight in a gentlemanly way." That seemed to sum up the attitude of both Virginia universities, and the other Southern schools wanted no part of it. Rather

Running back Sam Maphis, the captain of the 1924 Virginia squad, played for the Cavaliers from 1921-24. (UVa Sports Info)

than deal with Miles, these aggressive teams broke off and formed their own new conference, the Southeastern.

Henry "Puss" Redd, a former Tech player and assistant coach who also had a reputation as an English scholar and worked at the school as the alumni secretary, was named the head football coach for the 1932 season. He echoed Miles' beliefs in a campus speech, telling the student body, "We must win like true sportsmen, we must lose like true sportsmen. To me nothing is more discouraging than to see a young man perform brilliantly on the athletic field and then at the end of his college year fail to earn a diploma with his class."

Strangely, in the midst of this debate over the proper emphasis for athletics, Virginia Tech produced a great

Tech tackle Maggie Starke closes in on a ball carrier in the 1929 game at Charlottesville.

Tech's Mac McEver carries the ball against Virginia at Lambeth Field in Charlottesville in 1929.

team, made up of what McEver called "smart kids, not really athletes." Whatever their composition, the Hokies produced an 8-1 season that included victories over Georgia at Georgia, Kentucky, and Maryland. In their only loss, they fell to Alabama 9-6 in Tuscaloosa.

Although they didn't have scholarships, the Hokies did produce numbers by opening up tryouts among the corps of cadets in 1931, giving Redd a squad of 65 or 70 to work with. It was clearly the largest in Tech history. But the new coach whittled that number down to a traveling squad of 24, of which only 18 played regularly. Redd organized them in an oblong, military huddle, from which the players broke to the line while crisscrossing paths. Once in position, they called their plays crisply and moved the offense along at a brisk pace. The team, the season, was a model of efficiency.

"When I look back on it, I don't know how we did

it," said E.R. "Red" English, a guard on the 1932 club. "The thing we had was tremendous speed." Bill Grinus, a Midwesterner who earned academic honors in chemical engineering, and Bill Porterfield, a sophomore from Saltville, gave Tech a tough defense. Al Casey, a junior running back, was the most talented athlete on the team, but he didn't even start. With the strength—he could do fifty one-armed pushups—and the speed to be an All-American, Casey was a dynamic scoring threat as a substitute. But his unbridled spirit and confidence concerned the coaches. As a high school player in Petersburg, he once bragged to a Washington, D.C., newspaper reporter that he was going to score five touchdowns against a Washington-area team, and then did it. He was a shifty runner, English recalls. "I loved to block for him." His ability to pass and punt gave the team the triple threat it needed.

The Hokies ran off six straight wins, then lost to Alabama, the 1931 Rose Bowl champion. From there, they returned home to face Virginia in Blacksburg on a nasty afternoon, following a week of cold November rain. Heavy winds off the New River made passing and punting risky.

Virginia had compiled a 4-3 record, mostly on the strength of its defense, which the Wahoos used to keep Tech scoreless for most of the first half. Virginia relied on several goal line stands and the punting of quarterback Tommy Johnson. But those circumstances finally caught up with them just before the half when the Wahoos found themselves pinned near their own goal and forced to kick into the stiff wind. The ball traveled only to their 32, and from there the Hokies hit the only two successful passes of the day, setting up a dive by halfback George Smith.

The gusts did let up long enough for the Wahoos to complete a 17-yard pass in the fourth quarter, their only first down of the day. Otherwise, the afternoon belonged to Tech's ground game—253 rushing yards. The Hokies finished the scoring with a drive in the last period for the final margin, 13-0.

The Wahoos finished with just 11 yards rushing, 36 in total offense. Tech closed out a grand season with a 26-0 thrashing of VMI on Thanksgiving day, but it would prove to be the last hurrah for either program for the rest of the decade. The big times for both schools had passed. Eight seasons of tiresome mediocrity set in, and they tried to muddle their way through.

Typical of this era was Virginia's 1935 team, which finished with four scoreless ties, including a forget-

Staige Blackford played tackle and captained the 1923 Wahoo squad. (UVa SI)

table matchup with Tech, witnessed by only 2,500 spectators. That same season *College Topics* published the following inside joke:

"Are you attending the game today?" one Wahoo asked.

"Why, you don't attend games, you attend funerals," replied another.

"Well, they're all the same here at Virginia."

The series, however, did produce sporadic excitement, even if it was laughable at times. Lambeth Field was a sloppy, muddy mess for the 1933 game, and Virginia held a 6-0 lead until the final two minutes, when Tech drove to the Wahoos' five. Twice Tech ran a dive play for no gain. Then Puss Redd called on backup fullback Jim Ottoway. Virginia captain Ray Burger first grabbed Ottoway, *College Topics* reported, but he "spun clear, ran into Johnny Dial, smashed him out of the way, then got under Gene Wager . . . and carrying Gene, Burger, Dial, and several others, Ottoway took it over to tie the score."

Now, all Tech needed was an extra point from Red Negri to win it, except that Negri "hurried the kick off on a tangent" and not only missed, but missed quite badly, leaving the 'Hoos 'n' Hokies in yet another tie.

In 1934, George Smith scored three touchdowns to lead the Gobblers to a 19-6 win. And in 1936, the Cavaliers suffered another late loss when Tech scored on a freakish tipped pass play in the third quarter and uncharacteristically hit the conversion for a 7-6 margin.

The close losses only deepened the despair in Charlottesville. The school impaneled a committee to study its football failures and decided in 1936 to

The Cavaliers struggled to a 6-0 victory over the Hokies in the 1924 contest played in Blacksburg at Miles Field. The lone score of the game occurred when UVa's W. H. Ahner returned a fumble 40 yards for a score.

withdraw from the Southern Conference in hopes that an independent status would give Wahoo coaches more freedom to sign athletes to scholarships.

Somehow, VPI had managed despite the tightening restrictions of the conference. In their last nine games against Tech, the Wahoos were 0-6-3. After running through a series of coaches in the 1930s, the Wahoos brought in Frank Murray in 1937, who sought to reverse the losing trend by having his team practice at midnight the week before the VPI game. The Cavaliers stumbled about the field with only illuminated tape on the ball to light their way.

Murray also broke out new uniforms for the game. "The jerseys are woolen, of a burnt orange color, with large blue numbers on front and back" *College Topics* reported, "and one wide and two narrow blue circles around the arms. The pants are of the whipcord variety with little blue piping down the sides." The uniforms were "bought for their ability to withstand hard

knocks," the paper added. Goodness knows there had been plenty of those for the Wahoos.

But it was all to no avail.

That Saturday, the Hokies won again, 14-7, on another late-game play, this time a 26-yard pass.

Once again, the field was muddy. Once again, the crowd was light in Charlottesville—this time only 7,000, though the witnesses included the governor and many members of the General Assembly.

Murray finished 2-7 for 1937. Dreary as it seemed, things were already on the upswing. Midnight practices notwithstanding, the little man from Marquette could coach. More important, he could recruit. And he wasn't above looking beyond the private schools to find players. In fact, he even headed out into the coalfields, right in the Hokies' backyard, and found a star to brighten the Wahoos' path. In a very short time, the Virginia boys would find that they were no longer dancing in the dark.

Bullet Bill Dudley

BULLETPROOF AND BEYOND

"Dudley is the first Virginian who ever made Collier's All-American, and he rode with the spirit of the Cavaliers that came from the inspiration of Jeb Stuart, who forgot the odds."

—Grantland Rice, *Collier's Magazine*, 1941

Fortunately, Frank Murray had spent his formative years in the north, at Harvard and Marquette. Otherwise, he would have understood that University of Virginia coaches didn't take recruiting trips out to the coalfields. If Murray had been a son of Old Virginia, he might not have moseyed out to Bluefield during the summer of 1938 in a hunting expedition for athletes. And then he might not have found a skinny little back with average speed, a mediocre arm, and an awkward kicking style.

He might not have found William "Bullet Bill" Dudley— Everybody's All-American; NFL Rookie of the Year, All-Pro and leading rusher, 1942; NFL Most Valuable Player and leading rusher, 1946; Pro Football Hall of Famer, 1966.

His resume contains much more, of course, but those are the big items. Obviously, they were bigger than anything the state of Virginia had seen before—or since.

He demonstrated such obvious superiority on the field that, in 1941, when he personally destroyed the University of North Carolina at Kenan Stadium in Chapel Hill, the Tar Heel players were so overcome they helped Dudley's Virginia teammates carry him off the field.

"He's one of the greatest triple-threat backs I have ever seen," remarked the University of Tennessee's General Bob Neyland, the heavyweight coach of that era.

The five-foot, nine inch, 170-pound Bill Dudley didn't start out big. In fact, when he started playing football at Graham High School at age 14, his feet were so small the school didn't have shoes to fit him. That didn't matter. Before long, he

Coach Jimmy Kitts with two of the leaders of the 1941 Tech squad, Bill Tate (left) and Bill Zydiak.

was running the show.

"Bill always selected plays and handled tactics on the field—I never did," Marshall Shearer, his high school coach, once recalled. "On one occasion when we were playing North Fork, Bill and I were surveying the field, which was a lurch cut out of the mountainside. There was a seeping spring on the six-yard line, about 15 yards in from the sideline."

Shearer and Dudley decided that he should aim a punt for the puddle in hopes that it would cause North Fork to fumble. Sure enough, Dudley aimed for and hit the puddle dead center. The ball landed with a splash, and the officials ruled it dead. But then, as team captain, Dudley allowed the ref to move the ball out of the puddle to the center of the field. His coach was infuriated at this display of sportsmanship. "I kept muttering, 'At the half, I want to get ahold of Dudley,'" Shearer recalls.

But later, just before the half, North Fork fumbled in the middle of the puddle, and Graham recovered. The officials huddled and decided to move the ball to the center of the field, out of the water and right in front of the goal, where Graham got an easy score to win a close game.

"Now," Shearer's assistant coach asked as the officials moved the ball, "what are you going to say to Dudley?"

Those who coached him and played with him said Dudley had a vision and a football intelligence that, combined with a strong competitiveness, made him the unusual force that he was.

Looking for a nickname, the sportswriters of the era dubbed him "Bullet Bill" or the "Bluefield Bullet," but that was a misnomer, Dudley admits. "I wasn't very fast. In fact, there have been more articles written about how slow I was."

His speed, though, was deceptive—he had a great burst for the first 20 yards of any sprint. Besides, football is all about getting to the goal line, and Dudley always found a way to do that, leading the nation in scoring in 1941, his senior season.

His talent, prodigious as it was, was well hidden in 1938 in little Bluefield, a distant corner of the state tucked against the West Virginia line. Lacking the money to pay his way through college, Dudley hoped for a football scholarship. But Tech, VMI, and Washington and Lee all turned him down, pointing out that

he was a little on the small side.

Then, Dr. Jack Whitten, a family friend and state legislator from nearby Tazewell, called Dudley one summer evening and introduced him to Murray, who was in town scrounging for athletes. The Virginia coach figured at the least Dudley was a solid kicker and offered a $500 grant-in-aid, enough to cover room, board, and tuition in those days. Murray said Dudley could keep the scholarship as long as he remained eligible to play football.

That proved to be problem enough. "Virginia was a wonderful school," Dudley said, recalling the demanding instructors his freshman year. Fortunately, freshmen weren't allowed to compete on the varsity, and Dudley, just 16 years old, found the time to improve his academics.

Murray, meanwhile, busied himself with a varsity that showed signs of improvement for 1938, particularly since he had had the benefit of a second season to teach his "loose wingback" offensive scheme. "Anything can be expected of a Murray-coached ball club," *College Topics* observed that September.

The 1938 schedule marked the fiftieth anniversary of the school's football program, and to celebrate, the athletic department planned a special ceremony before the season opener with VMI. Enthusiasm, however, could not have been lower. "Until very recent years," *College Topics* offered in an editorial, "it was the custom, even further—the tradition here, to hold parades, rallies, and anything else to show the students' appreciation of their fighting men and teams."

But a decade of mediocre squads had killed football spirit on the campus, and while Murray seemed like a nice, scholarly man, no one was sure he could create a revival in Charlottesville. When the Wahoos opened the 1938 season with a 1-1-1 record, it seemed like more of the same.

One certain sign of the decline was the series record with VPI. Where once the Wahoos had held a commanding lead, the Hokies had drawn even with their 1937 win, bringing the standing to 11-11-3. "Never, since its dedication in 1926, have the Cavaliers succeeded in defeating the Gobblers on their home field," *College Topics* reported. "As a matter of fact, the Virginia tally sheets fail to show one win over the VPI team in 11 years. Much as we hate to say it, it would appear that the drive and zip of the student body in

Virginia star Bill Dudley, a member of the Professional Football Hall of Fame, scampers for yardage in a 1941 contest.

backing their team is slipping."

Just the opposite seemed to be the case in Blacksburg that October of 1938. It was Tech's Homecoming, and when the Wahoo players arrived for the game Saturday morning, they were greeted by a dead Cavalier hanging in front of the Student Activity building. Attached was a sign that read:

> *Here lies the bier*
> *Of the Cavalier*
> *He died in a wreck*
> *At Va. Tech*

As it turned out, the epitaph for Virginia's football program was a bit premature. Murray found the revival he was looking for that afternoon, a 14-6 win that, according to *College Topics*, "shattered an 11-year session of Polytechnic domination."

The star was junior back Jimmy Gillette, who himself would go on to an NFL career. Making use of Murray's numerous fake plays and reverses, Virginia drove to a touchdown early in the second quarter, a scoring run by Gillette off a double reverse. He scored again with a nice display of broken field running in the third quarter to make it 14-0. Tech's only sustained drive of the day netted a fourth-quarter touchdown.

The Wahoos were ecstatic. As they left town that afternoon, the dead Cavalier was noticeably absent from the student center.

Virginia finished the year 4-4-1, and Murray's style was exciting enough to generate a spark of interest in Charlottesville, but the Cavs were far from over the hump. Dudley opened the 1939 season buried in the backfield depth charts, and Murray faced whispered complaints that his coaching was too conservative. The whispering stopped when the Wahoos built their record to 5-2 heading into their late November meeting with Tech at Scott Stadium. Tech was struggling at 3-4-1 and seemed a likely victim.

The Wahoos, though, fumbled the opening kickoff,

Above: Bill Dudley scoots by helpless defenders in 1940 action.

Below left: Dudley, who had his attempts to attend Tech rebuffed, poses.

Below right: Virginia coach Frank Murray with John Acree.

gave up a quick touchdown, and fell into a funk that sent them to a 13-0 loss. After sixteenth-ranked Carolina nailed them the following week 19-0, their bright start fizzled to a 5-4 finish.

It was a tough close for Murray, but he had reason to be optimistic. As the state's newspapers pointed out, Virginia had another excellent freshman team in 1939 that had slaughtered all the opposition. And Dudley had begun his emergence as a sophomore. "It was in the Navy game [a close loss] that most people became aware of the Bullet," *College Topics* reported. "Breaking away about midfield, Bill snaked his way through the Middie defense to notch the first Cavalier score. Most people had to refer to their scoreboards to tell who made the sensational run. Throughout the year, Bill's performances improved. In the Maryland game, with only minutes remaining to play, it was Dudley and Gillette carrying out the now famous Murray flanker play. The two of them fought from behind to push over two of the flashiest and quickest touchdowns to win the game for the Cavaliers at 12-7."

Although it wasn't apparent to the people in the stands, Dudley's leadership was already a factor for the team.

In the spring of 1940, as Murray was setting the fall schedule, he told his players that they could play University of Tennessee, a national power that would surely beat them, or a lesser school that would get them another win.

Murray put the point to a vote of the players, and Dudley talked his teammates into choosing Tennessee. Astonished, Murray asked his young back why he wanted General Neyland's Volunteers.

Because you want to play the best, Dudley replied.

From the very start, the 1940 campaign was Dudley's coming out party. Virginia opened by smashing Lehigh and upsetting Yale and Maryland on the road. He didn't enter the Virginia starting lineup until the Yale game, but by then he was already a crowd favorite and a headline feature. Writers across the state raved about his running, his passing, his defense, his kicking.

But then the Wahoos hit a downturn, losing to William and Mary and VMI heading into the Tech game. The 1940 meeting was the first scheduled for Foreman Field in Norfolk, where the Virginia players were taken aback when the Hokies failed to show for pregame warm-ups.

That could only mean that the Gobblers are rough and ready, Murray warned in the locker room before kick off.

On the first play of the second period, Tech's Rankin Hudson fired a 40-yard touchdown pass to Herb Thomas (who would go on to win the Congressional Medal of Honor during World War II). As often happened in those old Tech/Virginia games, somebody missed the extra point. But six points was enough. Behind Dudley's kicking, the Wahoos settled into another familiar defensive struggle and lost, 6-0. What had seemed like another promising start had turned into a 3-3 season. And the Wahoos still had to face Tennessee. The fifth-ranked Volunteers laid a 41-14 pasting on the Cavs, but Dudley stunned the sellout crowd with his intense play.

"The young athlete did everything but consume the hog's hide," the Knoxville paper reported, "and he probably would have done that if an injury hadn't forced him to the sidelines in the closing minutes of the game. When Dudley limped reluctantly from the battlefield near dusk, the crowd scrambled to its frozen puppies and paid the Cavalier a tribute such as is seldom heard at Shield-Watkins Stadium. For several minutes the customers remained standing, clapping, yelling, and whistling their appreciation. . . ."

His performance also thawed Charlottesville's coolness toward the program.

"His outstanding spirit and heart have won for him the admiration and respect of thousands in the short period of one football season," *College Topics* declared, "and realizing that he has another year, we expect greater things of him still."

Greater things did come, beyond what anyone could have imagined for the Cavaliers. First, Frank Murray happened to take in a pro football game at the end of the 1940 season, the NFL championship game in which the Chicago Bears used the T-formation to wax Sammy Baugh and the Washington Redskins, 73-0. The Virginia coach came away duly impressed and began planning alterations to the single-wing offense he had the Cavaliers running.

Dudley had played tailback in the single wing and was charged with doing all the passing and kicking in addition to carrying the ball. Playing him as a T-formation quarterback would have reduced his effectiveness, so Murray decided to install the T-formation and put Dudley at left halfback. When the Cavs needed to pass, the quarterback would simply shift at the last instant, allowing the center to shotgun snap the ball to Dudley.

It sounded like a hare-brained scheme, and several other college coaches around the state snickered at Murray's plans to use the T. It would take too long to teach it to the players, they said. The criticism was just another element in Murray's struggle to revive the program at Virginia. As has often been the case, Virginia fans didn't realize what they had in the colorful coach.

He had played baseball, not football, as an undergraduate at Tufts, then went to graduate school at Harvard. From there he worked as a newspaperman and then as a teacher for 10 years until he happened into the football coaching job at Marquette in 1922. With Art Guepe as quarterback, Murray's Marquette teams gained national prominence in 1934, 1935, and 1936, leading to his hiring at Virginia. Guepe followed him to Charlottesville as the backfield coach, and Murray further expanded the Cavalier coaching staff by adding Arthur Corcoran, an old pro who had

played for Jim Thorpe's Canton Bulldogs, and Ralph Heikkinen, a former All-American lineman from Michigan.

Murray ran the proceedings as a scholarly gentleman. "If he heard you using profanity, he'd say, 'Bill, that's the voice of an uneducated man,'" Dudley recalled with a chuckle. "He had a doctor's degree in philosophy and a master's in English.

"Sometimes Coach Murray could be very excitable during ball games. When he'd get excited, Guepe would try to calm him down."

Where most coaches found it easy to chew tobacco and use the gruff tactics of a drill instructor, Murray considered himself a teacher. "He had all the time in the world for young people who came into his office," Dudley said. "When you went in his office to talk, he would talk with that young man or boy for half an hour or 45 minutes and make that kid feel like he was on top of the world."

That's exactly where the Cavaliers found themselves after the 1941 season. Virginia rolled up in an offensive whirlwind, outscoring 10 opponents 279 to 42, and Dudley was the total, ultimate force at the center. A newspaper reporter once figured that modern teams would employ seven people to do the chores that the Bluefield Bullet did all by himself, but the more accurate number was nine. He was a passer, a running back, a safety, a punter, a place-kicker, kickoff specialist, punt returner, kickoff returner, and a coach on the field.

In 1941, as a 19-year-old senior, Dudley led the nation in scoring with 134 points (including 18 rushing touchdowns, 23 extra points, and one field goal), setting a new

The 50th reunion of the 1941 Virginia squad.

season record in the process. He was also the national leader in total yardage: 2,439.

He finished second in the nation in rushing yardage with 957 and threw for another 857 yards and 12 touchdowns and completed 54 percent of his attempts.

This individual performance drove the Cavaliers to their most heralded season. "Going into our senior year," Dudley recalled, "Coach Murray reminded us that we had never beaten VMI, VPI, and North Carolina. We beat all three and finished 8-1."

Hampden-Sydney and Lafayette were the early victims, but the Wahoos struggled with the T and showed a propensity to fumble, which cost them a two-point loss to Yale in the third game. They wouldn't fall again. They whipped Richmond and VMI and faced Tech again in Norfolk on November 1. "I remember everything about it," Dudley recalled. "The wind was blowing awfully hard."

So hard, in fact, that a Hokie punter kicked the ball from his own 25-yard line and had to retreat five yards to down it on his own 20, which was typical of Tech's day. Dudley rushed for 134 yards and two touchdowns, passed for 114 yards and two touchdowns, and scored a total of 16 points as the Cavs dominated, 34-0.

New Tech coach Jimmy Kitts, from Southern Methodist University, was dumfounded at the outcome. The Hokies had been 4-2 heading into the game, including an upset over nationally ranked Georgetown.

"The same old lovely story . . . ," *College Topics* cooed the following Monday, "Bounding Bill Dudley led the Cavaliers to a decisive victory."

Still, the paper added, near the end of the game "there were many mutterings to the effect that the only gentlemanly thing to do was to let them threaten once."

Virginia then whipped Washington and Lee and Lehigh, setting up a season ending showdown with North Carolina, the game which would cement Dudley's All-American credentials and lead to his being selected as the number one pick in the NFL draft the following spring.

In leading the Wahoos to a 28-7 win, Dudley rushed 17 times for 215 yards and scored three touchdowns (on runs of 67, 79, and three yards); he completed six of 11 passes for 117 yards; he punted eight times for a 39-yard average; as a safety he was all over the field, with key tackles to stop Tar Heel drives.

When it was over and Murray brought Dudley to the bench, the crowd of 25,000 stood in prolonged applause.

"He came; they saw; he conquered," wrote Chauncey Durden of the *Richmond Times-Dispatch*. Within the coming weeks Dudley would earn All-American honors from the Associated Press and the United Press International.

Although Virginia fans buzzed with bowl hopes, the school's athletic officials made it clear that exam schedules could not be altered for a postseason game. "There is absolutely no disposition on our part to consider any bowl feelers," Athletic Director Norton Pritchett declared.

So instead of a bowl, the Cavs had a "Ball."

In late November, athletic officials festooned Mr. Jefferson's famous Rotunda in banners and washed the dome with red flood lights for a "Victory Ball" honoring Dudley. Dignitaries and students alike danced to Carolina swing music played by Mike U'Rann and his Tar Heel band. At the close of the evening, University Center president Jack Waltz presented Dudley with a statuette.

"Gee, Jack, this is very nice and I really appreciate it," Dudley said as the orchestra and the crowd launched into a rendition of the "Good Old Song."

The next weekend, December 7, Dudley traveled to Washington to see his hero, Redskins quarterback Sammy Baugh, play football. During the game, the public address announcer repeatedly called various generals and admirals to emergency phone calls, casting an eerie atmosphere over the game.

The news was blacked out during the contest, but afterward Dudley learned that the Japanese had struck Pearl Harbor. Soon the entire country would be turned topsy turvy. Dudley himself would be sworn into the army air corps that next September, but would not have to enter the service until he had completed his first NFL season—during which he turned the perennial doormat Pittsburgh Steelers into a contender with a 7-5 record.

Dudley had relatives fighting the conflict and he was eager to join them. When they weren't fighting the war, however, many military leaders busied themselves compiling excellent sports teams, arguing that these teams were good for morale. So like many great athletes, Dudley went to the Pacific briefly, but he wasn't allowed near the action. He spent most of

Virginia's George Grimes poses with the ball.

the war playing for military teams.

The rush to fill the ranks with able-bodied men drained most colleges of athletes during the war, yet those schools with military training bases nearby were able to field teams. Murray lost 29 players to graduation and what he called "Uncle Sam scholarships," leaving the Cavaliers to suffer through a 2-6-1 season in 1942.

The Hokies, meanwhile, lost their coach, Jimmy Kitts, to the service, and the program fell in the hands of long-time Tech players-turned-coaches Mac McEver and Tex Tilson. They weren't optimistic about their prospects until their first few practices, when they realized they had a group of overachieving smart kids who wanted to play. "Some way or another, we jelled," recalled McEver. "I don't know how or why."

The Gobblers finished 7-2-1 and regained a step on the Wahoos at Foreman Field in Norfolk. Tech drove for a score to open the game, then got another early in the second half, moving the ball 80 yards in just three plays. Moments later, the Hokies got another score, after a short Virginia kick, to stretch their lead to 20-0.

In the fourth quarter, Turnbull Gillette got the Cavs' comeback started with his passing. Virginia scored twice but ran out of time, which was a fitting conclusion to the era.

So many people had run out of time under the pressing weight of the war. Tech closed down its football program for two years, while Virginia pieced together a team by borrowing players from nearby military training sites.

"Most of the good talent was off in the war," said former Wahoo quarterback and long-time alumni secretary Gilly Sullivan.

Indeed it was, and when the conflict was over, the boys who had gone off to war came home as hardened veterans, if they came home at all. Colleges everywhere would be flooded with athletes going to school on the GI bill. This would prove to be a great boon to Virginia and a wretched curse for Tech. One would rise, while the other would sink.

The first indication of this came with revival of the series in 1945. The Cavs blitzed their way to a 7-0 start, including a 31-13 thumping of the Hokies, who could muster only a 2-6 season. The game was played in Roanoke's brand new Victory Stadium, where the series would make its home for most of the next decade.

With seven wins, there was talk of an Orange Bowl bid for the Wahoos, and even grudging talk that the team would accept it, in the face of faculty complaints that too much emphasis was being placed on athletics. When the Cavs lost their last two games, to Maryland and Carolina, the talk quieted.

The season proved to be Frank Murray's last at Charlottesville. He returned to Marquette for the 1946 season, taking his gentlemanly style with him and making way for his tough-guy assistant Art Guepe. There was a sense that Guepe would demand a discipline from his players that Murray never had the mind to instill. But that wasn't the reason many of the players were sorry to see Murray, by then in his sixties, leave.

"I fell in love with Coach Murray," recalled Sullivan, who came to Charlottesville in 1945 as a 16-year-old freshman. "He was a wonderful gentleman, a very intelligent person. He seemed to have a knack for developing a program utilizing the skills of the people he had. It was fun playing for him. We all like to do the things we do well."

The Wahoos had certainly done that under Murray. Hard as it seemed to believe in 1946, they were going to do the same—and more—under Guepe.

The Wahoos were about to get something they'd never had before. They were about to get an edge.

Defensive end Joe Palumbo was an All-American for the Cavaliers in 1951.

GUEPE'S MERCHANTS

> *". . . football will doubtless enjoy a great surge of popularity in post-war America. Men long keyed up and hardened by warfare will want a way to let off steam and ease off their razor-edged conditions."*

—*College Topics*, September 1945

In 1946, as the United States moved out from under the shadow of world war, the mood of the country shifted to boom. Economic boom. Housing boom. Baby boom. Entertainment boom. Even a football boom.

The end of World War II had brought the return home of hundreds of thousands of GIs. And money that had once been directed at the war effort suddenly began flowing into the American economy. First it was a trickle, then a rush. Sick of war bonds and weapons plants and rationing, people turned their thoughts to rebuilding their lives.

After five years of struggle and sacrifice, the public showed a vast hunger for fun. New products seemed to emerge overnight.

Virginia's Tom Scott.

Polaroid cameras. 33 1/3 long-playing records. Wash-and-wear shirts. Most fascinating of all was the television set, although there were only about 100,000 tubes (with seven- and 12-inch screens) in American households and bars in 1946. Even so, programmers were already looking to sports to snare the public's attention. A Joe Louis fight was aired in June 1946, and by 1947, the World Series would be telecast.

If things weren't new, they were at least innovative. Suddenly ice cream came in eight flavors, and Americans gobbled up 714 million gallons of it in 1946— much of it eaten, apparently, by pregnant women.

The biggest product, of course, was babies. Nearly 3.5 million were born in

1946 alone, and the numbers would spiral from there, blowing out all government projections on population. By the 1960s, there would be an extra 30 million Americans, all of them young and eager for excitement.

Looking back, it seems logical that big-time modern college football, itself a child of this baby boom, would grow and mature with the generation.

What doesn't seem logical is that Charlottesville would become a football hotspot after the war, and that Blacksburg would prove to be a chilling environment, as cold as the January wind blowing across the Tech parade field. But that's what happened.

The reason for the success in Charlottesville can just about be pinned on one man: Art Guepe, the strong, gruff guy who had starred as a quarterback for Frank Murray at Marquette, then joined him as an assistant coach at Virginia. When Murray returned to Marquette after the 1945 season, Guepe stayed behind to run the program.

Run it he did.

Where Frank Murray had been a fatherly sweetheart, Guepe was a stern, sometimes cold, taskmaster. The players used to say they knew when it was time for spring practice because Guepe would suddenly begin speaking to them.

Harold Hoak rumbled 46 yards for a touchdown in Virginia's 45-6 victory in 1950.

"He still had his youth," recalled Gilly Sullivan, who played his freshman year under Murray and his sophomore season under Guepe. "He physically was very strong, very fast himself. He could demonstrate the things he wanted done. He was more of a disciplinarian than Coach Murray. I was scared to death of Coach Guepe, to be honest with you."

"He was tough as hell," agreed end Bob "Rock"

Weir. "I didn't appreciate him until I left. He was one of the smartest guys to ever coach football."

Guepe, in a 1995 interview, chuckled at the recollection of his approach. "The boys might have thought I was tough because they couldn't do what they wanted," he said.

Yet, coaching in the postwar era required a special tolerance, and Guepe was far from unbending. In addition to the young players coming out of high school, many colleges were flooded with veterans returning from the war. Those schools with a nearby service program were well situated to snare that "veteran" talent, and Virginia, with a naval training program on campus, was one of those fortunate schools.

Many postwar players had been hardened by combat and military service. "They were special kids, or men," Guepe recalled. "We had to bow down a little bit to the older fellows. After all, you had to respect what they'd been through."

"It was a strange mix," Gilly Sullivan said. "There were young guys like me who had just missed the war, and there were some very experienced, mature men."

A classic example was Weir, who played two years at Princeton before the war and four years at Virginia afterward. "There were no rules in those days," Weir explained with a laugh. He had served two years in the South Pacific as a Marine rifle company commander and had been among the first American troops to occupy Nagasaki after the atomic bomb was dropped there.

Once he returned to the States, Weir wasn't shy about speaking his mind. This was evident in a game against North Carolina State. Weir played defensive end and had tackled a Wolfpack back for a safety. Just moments later, however, he did something that Guepe didn't like, so the coach brought him to the bench. They had a heated discussion, and Weir looked at Guepe and said, "You dumb sonofabitch."

"He made me sit for a long time that day," Weir recalled with a laugh.

While the war brought Guepe hard-minded players, it also brought him the offensive scheme that would make him the most successful coach in Virginia's history. He did his service time at the Iowa Preflight School, where the service team was experimenting with the split T-formation. Murray, of course, had begun experimenting with the formation at Virginia during the 1941 season, but it was Guepe's service experience that gave him a head start on the opposition once he returned to Charlottesville.

"That's what made our years at Virginia very special," Guepe recalled. "The other coaches for other teams didn't know anything about the split T."

Teaching the scheme was a challenge. Practices were tightly run skill and drill sessions. "There was no playing around and you'd better not be late," Weir recalled.

It didn't take long for the players to see how well the offense worked. Over the course of a game, Guepe would gradually spread his linemen farther and farther apart, and opponents' unwary defenses would shift

UVa greats, Coach Art Guepe and John Papit, watch the action on the field.

with them. "We created our own holes because the stupid defenses would go out with us," Weir recalled.

By the last two quarters, the spread formation meant that most blocks were merely brush blocks, which played right into the hands of Guepe's quick, hard-hitting style.

"Guepe was a coach you couldn't believe," recalled John Risher. "He wanted speed. He was quoted as saying he didn't care if his recruits could play football as long as they were fast. He could teach them to play football if they were fast."

"I favored speed," Guepe said, "but, of course, you couldn't be too choosy back then. You had to take what came along."

In those days, college coaches could put prospects through tryouts before offering scholarship aid. Weir recalled that he was the slowest man on the team, which meant that Guepe always lined the prospects up against him in a foot race. "If he couldn't beat me," Weir said with a laugh, "whoop, that kid was gone. They wouldn't look at him."

Guepe is carried off the field after one of his 47 career victories at Virginia.

Tech coach R.C. McNeish is flanked by Oren Hopkins (left) and Jack Ittner.

The speed allowed Guepe to set his quick backs even closer to the line in the T, which meant they hit the holes in a blink. Among the quickest was All-American John Papit, a blazing fullback who led the 1947-50 teams in rushing and set both the single-game record (224 yards against the powerful Washington and Lee team of 1948) and the season record (1,214 yards in 1949, which remained unbroken until Barry Word rushed for 1,224 yards in 1985). For 1949, he was named to the prestigious Newspaper Enterprise Association's All-America first team.

"Papit was a great ballcarrier, tremendous leg strength," recalled Gilly Sullivan. "Give him a little daylight and he was gone. He had speed and power."

Still, Papit didn't fit the traditional model of a fullback. "He could run with the wind," agreed Weir. "But he was one dimensional. He couldn't catch a pass, couldn't block. He'd get more damn concussions

trying to block people, so they wouldn't let him block anyone."

Guepe's teams were also strong defensively. With Weir at end was All-America nose guard Joe Palumbo, whose quickness often chilled opposing ball carriers before they left the backfield. Playing from 1949-1951, he earned Associated Press first team All-America honors.

"Joe would be on top of the quarterback before he knew what hit him," Weir said. "He was one of the greatest guards that ever played here. The guy was so quick it was unreal."

Guepe's first team struggled with the T-formation and finished 4-4-1, including a 21-21 tie with the Hokies. The Wahoos' scoring featured a 53-yard punt return by Ray Brown. But Tech's Ralph Beard finished off a late drive with a touchdown run to tie the game. The Hokies would go on to finish the year 3-3-3 and accept an invitation to the Sun Bowl (a Tech alumnus was influential in the selection), which they lost to Cincinnati.

That 1946 tie would be as close as Tech got to defeating a Guepe team. Over the next six seasons, the Wahoos would outscore the Gobblers, 219-13. In short, the Hokies lost it in the postwar years, compiling a 3-33-3 record from 1948-1951.

During that same period, Guepe's Wahoos ran up a 43-13-1 record in six seasons, including a 31-7 record from 1949-1952. This showing was unprecedented in Virginia's football history, and it stirred high feelings among the student body and alumni. "Here in Wahooland, where there's a coat and tie on every collegian, a crewcut and saddle shoes on almost all of the same, and 'Yankee Wastrels'—as Virginius Dabney calls them—dotting the grounds, there's an offensive football team abrewing that will cause other coaches around the state many a sleepless night before this fall draws to a close," crowed *College Topics*.

To a student body that numbered about 3,500, Virginia sold 2,000 student tickets in advance for the 1947 Tech game in Roanoke's Victory Stadium. Yet, many in the University community were clearly troubled by what was perceived as too much emphasis on football.

"We didn't let that bother us," Guepe recalled.

Indeed.

The 1947 Cavs, with 27 lettermen stocking their ranks, ran off a 7-3 record and whipped Tech 41-7, with a host of backs scoring and running up nearly 500 yards in offense before the crowd of 22,000. Halfback Grover Jones scored early on a 28-yard run, and the Wahoos steadily moved the ball behind the triple threat of 23-year-old George Grimes. Late in the game, the Cavs would have been content to run out the clock, except that Hokie Cordell McCraw blocked a punt and scored. To answer, the Cavs drove the kickoff for yet another touchdown, a toss from backup quarterback Joe Black to freshman Ed Bessell.

"We were ready and we struck early," Guepe said with satisfaction.

Tech coach Jimmy Kitts was stunned. "I didn't think it would be like this," he told reporters.

The next year, the Cavs dipped to 5-3-1, but they still blanked Tech, 28-0 in a game that featured a 57-yard pass play to Weir and a 65-yard run by Papit.

Back Floyd Tayloe scored twice, and Virginia fans were so excited that early the next week they purchased 4,000 advance tickets to the Princeton game, "the largest opening day sale in University history," according to *College Topics*.

For 1949, Guepe had so much talent on hand he moved to a two-platoon system. Virginia finished 7-2 and beat the Hokies 26-0 at impossibly muddy Victory Stadium. "About the only department in which Tech excelled," *College Topics* noted, "was the quality of its band, which dazzled some 15,000 fans with a brilliant halftime exhibition." In an attempt to improve their plight, the Hokies had held a brief scrimmage before the game "to see who really wanted to play," which left *College Topics* wondering if the Gobblers "hadn't used up all their energy because their attack went for nil against a solid Cavalier forward wall."

The Wahoos pushed their record to 7-0 before losing close games to Tulane and North Carolina, which were tied for the nineteenth ranking in the Associated Press poll. Regardless, the taste of the big time only drove Guepe and his staff harder. During each game, the coach would kneel on the sideline, chain-smoking cigarettes and following the action closely.

George Grimes catches a 34-yard pass in a 41-7 Wahoo victory in 1947.

Tech's Ballard closes in on Billy Pennell of UVa in 1947 action.

Each year, the drubbing of Tech seemed to get worse. "They were pitiful," Weir recalled. "Art used to get madder 'n hell because we couldn't get pumped up to play them."

On the bus ride to Roanoke each year, Guepe would preach that Tech could be dangerous, but his players would snicker. "We didn't worry about VPI," Weir said. "We knew we'd beat 'em 40-0. We always played down in Victory Stadium down in Roanoke back then, which fit in with their farmer image. They never cut the grass; they let cows graze all over that field. There was cow flop everywhere. It was amazing."

"We didn't have much trouble with the Gobblers," Guepe admitted.

With so many veterans tired of military service, it had been hard for the Hokies to attract older athletes to their cadet corps. "They just didn't get the players anymore," Guepe said.

The 41-7 thrashing by the Wahoos in 1947 had the Gobbler alumni calling for coach Jimmy Kitts' resignation, which he promptly gave them. In Kitts' footsteps came R.C. McNeish, a former star halfback at Southern Cal, who won one game in three seasons.

The protracted losing streak had Tech alumni screaming that a student aid foundation should be formed to raise money for athletics. Puss Redd, the former Tech coach, attempted to block them. But with the losses mounting, the alumni proceeded with their fundraising plans without waiting for Redd's consent.

Meanwhile, Guepe's Cavs kept pounding the Hokies. With All-American and eventual Hall of Famer Tom Scott leading the way, Guepe's 1950 team went 8-2 and whipped Tech 45-6. Virginia led 7-0, when Tech's Sterling Wingo surprised the crowd with an 84-yard punt return for a touchdown, but the Cavs quickly shut the Hokies down thereafter. The Cavs rang up 28 first downs and 481 yards of total offense. "Yet the team was not overly sharp," *College Topics* complained afterward. For Virginia's sixth touchdown, back Harold Hoak bulldozed his way down the center of the field for 46 yards, running over every shell-shocked Hokie in his path.

The next season, the Cavs went 8-1 and drubbed the Hokies, 33-0, with a number of young backs eager to show they could replace Papit. Virginia's only loss came against national power Washington and Lee.

That year, 1951, the university commissioned a committee, chaired by professor Robert Gooch—himself a footballer from the early 1900s—to study the role of athletics at Virginia. The committee's findings, known as the Gooch Report, concluded that the school had gotten caught up in "big-time athletics," and the committee called for a de-emphasis of sports, particularly football.

The day before the game against Washington and Lee, the controversial report about the University's athletic program was released. The findings outraged many alumni and set off an immediate debate on campus. Perhaps the Wahoos were distracted that next day as Washington and Lee won

their showdown, 42-14, the only time the Generals beat a Guepe team.

In 1952, with Scott as a senior, Virginia went 8-2 and downed Tech, 42-0. The game was clearly over by halftime, with the last two quarters given to subs from both teams to finish out the clock. About the only excitement was a brief fisticuffs, *College Topics* reported. "Both squads swarmed onto the field, but were peaceably shooed off again by the officials."

The Wahoos lost one game to sixth-ranked Duke and another to South Carolina. The close of the campaign ended a remarkable three-year stretch in which they'd won 24 and lost five. "We had a definite advantage in our scheduling," Guepe said modestly. "We played teams that didn't have GIs like we did."

The success seemed garish to many on the Virginia faculty. "It appeared to me that the administration of the University itself wasn't all that excited about a

John Papit is second on the Cavaliers' career rushing list.

Johnny Papit breaks into the open field
with the Cavaliers up 7-0.

successful athletic program," observed Gilly Sullivan, who worked for decades in Virginia's alumni office. "The changes and transactions over the long pull turned out to be very negative."

Like Tech, the University of Virginia was struggling with its approach to the increasingly commercial business of college sports. The two schools answered the question by heading in opposite directions, as they had done so often.

Virginia's first step toward a period of losing and mediocrity came after the 1952 season, when the university administration allowed Guepe to leave for Vanderbilt University. "Art asked for a raise," Weir explained. "They were paying him $9,000 per year, so they said they'd give him $9,500. And he said, 'The Hell with you,' and went to Vanderbilt for $12,000."

"I didn't let it bother me," recalled Guepe, who went on to serve Vanderbilt 21 seasons as a head coach.

However, few in Virginia's camp realized how stark and dramatic the

school's athletic decline would be, with losing season following losing season. Tech, on the other hand, was headed back up. A take-charge guy named Frank Moseley was the new coach in Blacksburg, and although he had to suffer through some miserable losses, he was tough enough to see it through and turn things around. Soon his teams would enjoy the superiority that Guepe's had known.

Meanwhile, Saturday afternoons in Charlottesville became bitter, frustrating affairs, and the men who had played for Guepe would leave Scott Stadium week after week shaking their heads. Losing to Virginia Tech became such a regular event that Gilly Sullivan made up a story. He told people that he had a six-year-old son who cried when Virginia finally beat Tech again in 1957.

"All he had known all his life was losing," Sullivan told people. "He didn't think that Virginia was supposed to win."

Above and opposite: **Rock Weir was a Wahoo defensive stalwart during Guepe's tenure.**

Carroll Dale shows the pass-catching form that made
him one of the Hokies' all-time greats.

HOKIES HIGH

CHAPTER 5

"There was a time when we didn't even have to worry about scouting them."

—Evan J. "Bus" Male, Virginia player and coach

If the Virginia Tech Hokies needed anything in 1951, it was a tough son of a gun to straighten out their football program. Frank O'Rear Moseley perfectly fit that bill. He put fire in the eyes of the defeated and fear in the hearts of the weak. There were plenty of both in Tech's football program when he arrived in Blacksburg.

He was aloof and hard-nosed, yet he somehow communicated to his players that he cared for them. He was a demanding patriarch whose grueling practices left his players cursing him bitterly.

"Moseley used to just run us to death," recalled Don Divers, who played fullback from 1954-1956. "He was brought up in the old line. He told you what he expected. You either did it or got the hell out."

As coach and athletic director, he was the guid-

Dick Voris was able to win only one game in his three-year stint as the Cavaliers' head coach.

ing force behind Virginia Tech football for more than a quarter century. He came to Blacksburg armed with the verve that would carry the program from winless misery to the age of big-business college athletics.

Considering Moseley's credentials, Tech was damned lucky to get him. The Blacksburg job wasn't just another career stepping stone for Frank Moseley. He dedicated his professional life to the school. He was a model young coach and executive, germinated in the same ground that produced Bear Bryant. He and The Bear played together, even briefly roomed together, at the University of Alabama in the early thirties. Later, he became an assistant to Bryant, first at Maryland, then Kentucky. Moseley was working for Bryant in 1950 when Tech president, Dr. Walter S. Newman, heard about him.

Actually, Newman and

the athletic council were interested in another of Bryant's assistants at Kentucky, Carney Laslie. Laslie turned down the offer to become Tech's head coach, but recommended Moseley.

That December, Newman and two members of the athletic council interviewed Moseley for four hours, questioning his philosophy while trying to gauge his intensity. They reasoned that Moseley, at 39, had ample experience, and he convinced them he could make VPI a winner. At the end of the session, they offered him the longest and most lucrative contract ever for a Tech coach, about $10,000 annually for five years.

Ben Martin coached the 1956-57 editions of the Cavalier football team.

Gus Tebell coached the Wahoos for three seasons.

Moseley, who had helped develop Kentucky's famed quarterback, Babe Parilli, stayed with the Wildcats through their New Year's upset of Oklahoma in the Sugar Bowl. Then he got in his car and drove straight through to Blacksburg. In the hills of Western Virginia he found a decided contrast to the Sugar Bowl champions he had just left. The Tech players seemed shell-shocked by three years of defeat.

"The material situation, as far as I'm concerned, is very discouraging," Moseley wrote in his first exclusive *Student Aid Association newsletter*. "Much money has been spent and very little or no value received. At present, we have about fifty freshmen, sophomores, and juniors on football scholarships, costing about $40,000 per year, and in my way of thinking, only 21 of the 50 have any possibilities at all."

After looking at his players in spring practice, Moseley wrote, "They have a decided injury complex, as if they had been put through a meat grinder (they seem to fear going through it again), but I suppose if you or I had lost as much as they have we would feel the same way."

Moseley dubbed his rebuilding program "Operation Bootstrap." Jack Prater, who later headed Tech's Student Aid Foundation, was a sophomore during Moseley's first season at Tech. Those first few months of Moseley's program, many players went to "the war," Prater said. Not the Korean War, but the war that Moseley waged on Tech's losing attitude.

It would be a bit of an understatement to say the new coach raised the level of intensity. Only the tough survived. Most didn't. "Under the cover of darkness,

guys left here so fast they ran over each other," Prater recalled. Of the 26 scholarship football players in the class of 1953, only three finished their playing eligibility.

Keeping one eye on his football team, Moseley, as athletic director, also had to take the long view. He resolved that by reasoning if the school had a good football team, its other sports programs would improve as well. The school itself was adrift without an identity in those years following World War II, caught in a flux between the small military college it had been and the large state university it was becoming. Moseley sensed that if his football program was successful, it could serve a useful role in fusing that identity.

Some months before Moseley's arrival, alumni director Puss Redd dropped his opposition to raising funds for athletics from alumni. When a group, including Red English and E.R. Lane, of the Lane Company in Altavista, formed the Virginia Tech Student Aid Foundation in 1949-1950, Redd gave them a list of about 5,000 possible alumni donors. From his business office in Altavista, English addressed and mailed the letters soliciting contributions for athletics.

By the time Moseley arrived in 1951, the group had raised almost

$10,000. The foundation members and other Tech supporters were eager to meet the new coach and present him with the money. They got that chance in a meeting at a Roanoke hotel not long after Moseley arrived, English recalled. "I got up in front of the group and gave my little song and dance about how hard we had worked for it. When I got through, Moseley said, 'If that's all you got, just keep it.' He shocked that crowd into giving about $9,000 more that night."

Despite the conditions and the losing record, Moseley announced that he would make Tech a winner within five years. Having made the promise, he went to work recruiting tirelessly, speaking at high school banquets and alumni gatherings across Virginia and West Virginia, never missing the opportunity to extoll the good of athletic scholarships. His message was clear: Big-time athletics is nothing to fear. A winning image would provide a common thread for the university. That was exactly what the school's officials and alumni wanted to hear.

The newspapers liked it as well. Reporters wrote about this new fellow Moseley, son of a cop from Montgomery, Alabama. Nicknamed "Chesty" from his school days. One tough cookie. A winner.

He identified and pursued the talent in the region. Among that first group of players were George Preas,

Above: Frank Moseley doles out instructions.

Below: The undefeated 1954 Hokie team went 8-0-1.

Above right: Tech legends Frank Moseley and Carroll Dale. (Photo Virginia Tech Sports Information)

Above: Billy Kerfoot was a co-captain of the undefeated 1954 team.

Below left: Guard John Polzer played at UVa. from 1953-55.

Below: Tom Petty caught nine touchdown passes for Tech's 1954 squad.

Tom Petty, and Billy Kerfoot, who would later earn All-Southern Conference honors. Then the staff recruited a young quarterback prospect, Johnny Dean, away from the University of Virginia. That left the Wahoos fuming. Dean, from Tidewater, was one of the most highly recruited players on the East Coast. Yes, the reporters decided, this Moseley would raise the level of intensity across the state.

Although the budget was tight, the coaches had enough money to bring in 19 freshmen on scholarship. Eventually, it would prove to be a golden group.

The Hokies won that first game of the 1951 season, against Marshall, breaking their 10-game losing streak—only to resume it over the next seven weeks, as Davidson, Virginia, George Washington, Duke, North Carolina State, Washington and Lee, and William and Mary pounded them mercilessly by a combined score of 355-60. Tech beat Richmond and lost to VMI to finish that first Moseley campaign at 2-9.

But the players Moseley had gathered from across the region paid immediate dividends, and the 1952 team finished 5-6, with wins over Marshall, Davidson, The Citadel, Richmond, and VMI. Just before the 1953 season, school officials gave Moseley a new eight-year contract. His pay didn't increase, but the job security did, reflecting the new confidence on campus.

For Moseley the athletic director, 1953 brought another great challenge. Seven schools—Wake Forest, Duke, North Carolina State, North Carolina, South Carolina, Clemson, and Maryland—broke away from the Southern Conference to form the Atlantic Coast Conference. The next year, the University of Virginia would join the new league.

Moseley, a man of foresight, could see that, except for West Virginia and Tech, the remaining schools in the Southern Conference faced a future of lower-rung competition. Moseley began a 15-year campaign to join the ACC, but all of his advances were shunned. As Mac McEver explained, Tech's sports programs had become so weak in the late 1940s, the Hokies weren't considered for ACC charter membership. And by the time Moseley made Tech strong again, the ACC members decided they wanted to keep their club exclusive and small.

As for the Wahoos, they weren't exactly secure in their new conference home. Athletic Director Gus Tebell had favored joining the ACC. University President Colgate Darden opposed the move, however, saying it placed too much emphasis on sports. The issue was settled ultimately by the Board of Visitors, who supported the move.

"I think an awful lot of people thought we were in over our heads in joining the ACC," Gilly Sullivan said.

Those feelings surfaced almost as soon as Art Guepe left Charlottesville. Assuming the Virginia head coaching duties was longtime assistant Ben McDonald, who had been a team captain at the University of Texas in the 1930s. McDonald and Guepe had met at the Iowa preflight program, and from there conducted their T-formation experiment together.

But where Guepe was hard-nosed, McDonald had a special gift with the players. "Ned was the most beloved coach that ever hit that campus," Rock Weir recalled. "He was something else. He'd come over and put his arm around you and say, 'Son, this is how it's done.'"

"The young people who played for him loved him," Gilly Sullivan agreed. "I'll never understand why it didn't work out for him here."

"Some men are meant to be president; some are meant to be vice president," Weir said.

Maybe McDonald was not the stern taskmaster needed to run a college football team, but Virginia's talent cycle had also run its course. Weir said 1953 was the first year he organized an alumni game, pitting the recent grads against the current team in a preseason contest. The alumni whipped the Virginia varsity 42-0 just days before the 1953 season opened against the Hokies.

"A win could get the team with their new coach and quarterback off on the right foot," College Topics observed, "while a loss might start the squad on a long backward march."

A long march backward it was. Cavs safety Eddie Knowles scored on a 56-yard punt return, but Tech backup quarterback Jackie Williams drove the Hokies to a 20-6 win, ending Virginia's decade of domination. The Wahoos would win narrowly over George Washington in their third game of the season, then lose every other contest to finish 1-8, a steep fall from the previous year's 8-2 record.

The Hokies, meanwhile, were rising. Going into the last game of the 1953 season against VMI, Tech had

Tech defeated the favored Cavaliers 14-7 in 1956. (Photo VT Special Collections)

a 5-4 record and seemed headed toward its first winning record in more than a decade.

Lane and English invited Owen Cheatham, the president of Georgia Pacific, to Roanoke to watch the game in hopes he would contribute a good sum to Tech athletics. English and Lane bragged about the program that day, about how Moseley had made Tech a winner. But as the game dragged on, it became clear the underdog Keydets were upsetting the Hokies. By the time the game ended, 28-13, Lane was furious. In a meeting the following week in Roanoke, he had a heated argument with Moseley. The furniture company president left the meeting intending to have the coach fired, but English talked him out of it on the trip back to Altavista, pointing to the immense progress the team had made. For the first time in almost a decade, they had broken free, finishing 5-5. After he calmed down, Lane agreed. The Hokies were frustrated by the years of losing, but they could sense that Moseley had his sights set on big things.

In a dramatic turn-

It appeared as if two Hokies were wide open on this play. (Photo VT Special Collections)

around, Tech rose as high as fourteenth in the 1954 Associated Press national rankings before finishing the year at sixteenth.

It was a dream squad, the fruit of Moseley's three years of hard recruiting. The 1954 Gobblers were small, swift, and smart. They were deep in talent at the skill positions. Even more important, from the coach to the water boy, they had a huge hunger for winning.

"Moseley was a heck of a taskmaster," Jack Prater recalled in a 1981 newspaper interview. "Losing? We had great desire in the unbeaten season. We were afraid of losing. Each game was like playing for life. We were in top physical condition to meet the challenge."

The first three entrees on the menu that fall were all Atlantic Coast Conference teams. True to their names, the Gobblers rushed through the first part of the schedule like gluttons, consuming North Carolina State, 30-21, Wake Forest, 32-0, and Clemson, 18-7.

Those first wins had special meaning, with Moseley and school officials desiring entry into the ACC. "The first thing you know, Tech will win the Atlantic Coast Conference championship," ACC Commissioner Jim Weaver jokingly told reporters in Charlotte before the Clemson game. Privately, Weaver was worried about the appearance of Tech dominating the league.

The season was barely under way before the newspapers began talking of an undefeated season. Moseley tried to put the sportwriters off, saying he thought his 1955 team would be the big one. But privately, "Mose" was delighted. He knew he had a solid core of experienced seniors to go with his unbelievable stable of underclassmen. The offensive line was veteran and used to working together.

The ends, Tom Petty and Bob Luttrell, as well as future Baltimore Colt George Preas at tackle, team captain Billy Kerfoot and Jim Haren at guard, John Dean at quarterback, and Howie Wright and Billy Anderson at halfback, were all seniors.

Prater, after a two-year hitch in the Army, returned to school looking for a role on the team. The coaches knew he was too good a player to leave on the bench, so they placed him at center-linebacker, where his nose for hard hitting would make a difference. Other juniors were halfback Dickie Beard, utility backfielder Leo Burke, and lineman Jim Locke. The sophomores included quarterback Billy Cranwell, center John Hall, end Grover Jones, and halfbacks Dave Ebert, Don Divers, and Bobby Wolfenden.

Seeking an offensive set to match the team's speed, Moseley shifted from the regular "I" formation to the split "I."

"We were not a big team," Prater said. "In fact, we hardly had a player weighing over 220 pounds. It was the era of racehorse football, and we fit the bill. Our players were tall and slender, with exceptional speed and agility. That was the key to our success. We were probably one of the fastest football teams in Tech history."

The squad was well versed in the fundamentals. Moseley had an excellent staff, with Buck Chapman, Alf Satterfield, H.M. McEver, and Dick Redding. The Hokies knew how to hit.

There was another, even larger, factor: chemistry. Leo Burke, who played fullback, halfback, and quarterback and went on to enjoy a career in professional baseball, said the key to the 1954 team was its closeness, "that family-type feeling, that togetherness. We still have it.

"Somehow these boys came together. There was never any animosity over who was getting playing time. When we went out on the field, we all went out together. Today, when we get together, it's not like seeing old friends. It's like seeing family."

The week after the Clemson win, Shirley Povich, the *Washington Post* columnist, adopted the Hokies as his team. "Oklahoma, No. 1, you may have," he wrote. "Take Notre Dame, and UCLA, and Purdue, and Maryland, and the other giants of college football as well . . . I'm choosing to suffer it out with my new heroes, the boys at VPI."

Povich said he liked Tech because it was a "reminder that college football is not all big-time stuff." The Hokie fans, of course, felt differently. For years the alumni had wanted a piece of the big-time. And Frank Moseley was finally taking them there.

They didn't quite go all the way that season. To have expected that would have been unrealistic. The Gobblers had been down so long, there wasn't much

Billy Holsclaw threw two touchdown passes and was responsible for 181 yards of offense in the 1958 game.
(VT Special Collections)

talk of bowl invitations. And the seniors on the team killed what little there was by making it known they weren't interested in going.

After a narrow win over Richmond, the Hokies met Virginia on October 23 in Victory Stadium. With 24 lettermen back, the Cavs faced a schedule that included four top-twenty teams, including Penn State. They would lose to three of them by a total of 11 points. Instead of a breakthrough season, Virginia finished 3-6, with the narrow losses taking away the confidence McDonald needed to build.

Cavalier Jim Bakhtiar dives in an attempt to tackle VPI's Bailey. (VT Special Collections)

One of the heartbreaks was a 6-0 loss to the Hokies. Tech's tally came on a twenty-yard pass from Billy Cranwell to sophomore end Grover Jones. The Cavs had driven right to Tech's goal line in the second period, but "didn't have that extra little bit to push the ball across," *College Topics* reported.

The next week Tech slipped against long time nemesis William and Mary, finishing in a 7-7 tie. They won their last three games for a final record of 8-0-1, the only postwar undefeated season by either Tech or Virginia.

Across the state, newspapers reported Moseley's dreams for a big athletic complex, with a 24,000-seat stadium, a coliseum, practice fields, a golf course and a baseball field. Moseley didn't like the idea that Tech had to play its big games in Victory Stadium in Roanoke.

Moseley had shown he could accomplish the remarkable: go from winless to undefeated in four short years. This left him with a new challenge: sustaining that success.

In 1932, the Hokies had climbed to the peak of big-time college football, only to retreat quickly into mediocrity. Now that they had made the ascent again, Moseley wanted to make sure it wasn't followed by another backslide. As coach and athletic director, he faced a difficult juggling act. He had to coach well enough to win, while continuing to build the program on a tight budget. In the middle of it all, he had to conduct a public relations campaign.

Strangely, the Tech student community hadn't responded all that warmly to this coach who had turned things around. For all its glory, Tech's 1954 team enjoyed little support from the cadet corps. Something of a rift had developed between the scholarship athletes Moseley brought in and the student body.

For the most part, the misunderstanding was a result of the growth in Tech's civilian student population. For some cadets, the football team was a symbol of the changing face of Virginia Tech. With thousands of civilians gaining admission in the decade after the war, the corps could sense that it had lost control, that its existence was threatened. Moseley held a meeting with cadet leaders after the 1954 season to discuss ways of improving the situation.

His communication with the students was reflected in a slightly better reception the next fall. Gauged by the letters and columns in *The Virginia Tech*, the school's students slowly acquired a greater appreciation of the football team over the next few years. Still, the relationship was an uneasy one.

Throughout the period, the editions of *The Virginia Tech* featured varying criticisms and defenses of Moseley from the numerous Monday-morning quarterbacks in the corps. The students, in their youth, really weren't aware of the challenges Moseley faced and didn't appreciate what he had accomplished. Moseley was stoic; the situation only served to make him all the more determined.

In 1955, the Gobblers finished 6-3-1, and while Virginia had high hopes with sensational sophomore fullback Jim Bakhtiar and All-ACC guard/linebacker John Polzer, the Wahoos only plunged lower, falling to 1-9 and 0-4 in the ACC. The Cavs actually led Tech in their October meeting in Roanoke, 13-10, but in the third period, Hokie tackle Pat Carpenito blocked a punt and recovered the ball on the one-foot line. Tech quarterback Leo Burke scored three plays later to give the Hokies their third straight win in the series, 17-13.

The season brought the end of McDonald's painful tenure, and he was replaced by Ben Martin, a 1945 graduate of the Naval Academy. His 1956 team would finally bring the Wahoos an ACC win, 7-6 over Wake Forest. Three weeks later, the Cavs met sixteenth-ranked Tech in Roanoke. The Hokies were led by flashy quarterback Jimmy Lugar, halfback Bobby Wolfenden, and a young end with a big future named Carroll Dale. Tech back Ray England ran 44 yards for a touchdown in the first quarter. Virginia quarterback Nelson Yarbrough led a passing drive to tie the game at 7-all. A Tech touchdown in the third put the Hokies back on top, and they held on for a 14-7 win.

The Hokies finished the year as the number two rushing offense in the nation, with 2,835 yards, just behind Oklahoma. That December, the honors again rolled in. Lugar was named to the All-Southern Conference first team, and John Hall won the Jacobs Blocking Trophy. Moseley was named Southern Conference Coach of the year, and *Coach and Athlete Magazine* named him regional coach of the year.

In the middle of Moseley's conservative, run-oriented offense was another nugget of gold—freshman Carroll Dale had led the team with eight receptions for 157 yards and three touchdowns. A surprising number of people were taking notice of that.

The September 7, 1957 edition of the *Saturday Evening Post* tabbed Dale as the top sophomore lineman in the nation. Dale realized every ounce of his potential, first at Tech, then in a very successful pro career. Although Tech fielded only average teams, at best, after Dale's freshman season, he became Tech's first All-American.

He was raised in Wise, in the Virginia coalfields, where he starred in football, basketball, and baseball at J.J. Kelly High School. He was headed to the University of Tennessee, until the Tech coaches coaxed him away. In a surprisingly quiet and efficient manner, he became the school's premier football player.

He stood six-feet-two, 197 pounds, and was the fastest player on the Tech team. He pushed his immense physical skills to the limit, with a penchant for hard work. After his junior season, 1958, he was

named the Southern Conference Player of the Year and a second-team Associated Press All-American. His senior year, he was named first team All-American by *LOOK* magazine's Football Writers and the Newspaper Enterprises Association (NEA), and first-team All-Conference. The Associated Press repeated its error of 1958, naming him to the second team.

Dale was invited to the Blue-Gray Game and the Senior Bowl. Later that year, as a member of the college all-star team, he played against the NFL champions, the Baltimore Colts, whose offensive line was studded with two former Tech greats, Buzz Nutter and George Preas.

In the days of run-oriented, conservative football, Dale became Tech's all-time leading receiver, with 64 receptions for 1,195 yards and 15 touchdowns. He made most of his catches under double- and triple-teaming. Because Tech never really had a full-fledged passing game to showcase his skills, he did the other chores, the team things. He was an exemplary blocker and tackler, earning the Jacobs Blocking Trophy both in 1958 and again in 1959.

Moseley beamed at the mention of Carroll Dale, but the opposing coaches sang his praises the loudest. Florida State's Perry Moss said, "We double-teamed him the whole game. YOU have to. He's a great athlete." West Virginia's Art Lewis said Dale "would play for anybody. We haven't seen a better end." After a frustrating day of watching his defensive backs try to stop Dale, North Carolina State's Earle Edwards told reporters, "Dale is going to make a lot of defensive halfbacks look bad. He has fooled the best of them."

His humility warmed even the cynicism of the newspaper writers. When, as a senior, Dale told them he valued his election as team captain as much as his other honors, they believed him.

He played his best ball in the NFL, where the creative offenses allowed his skill as a receiver to blossom. He was drafted by the Los Angeles Rams in 1960 and caught a touchdown pass in his first game as a pro. After five seasons with the Rams, he was traded to the Green Bay Packers, where he was a starter for Vince Lombardi on three straight championship teams. He was named to the Pro Bowl in 1970 and 1971. He made the game-winning reception in 1970.

Virginia also had a promising young player. Jim Bakhtiar, a native of Abadan, Iran, had come into the

1956 season touted as the best sophomore fullback in the nation by virtually every leading magazine. He had quickly become a favorite of Cavalier fans, who nicknamed him the "Persian Prince."

Despite Virginia's weak showing in 1956, Bakhtiar had carried the ball 203 times, while also doing his share of linebacking for the Cavs. If there was reason for optimism in Charlottesville heading into the 1957 season, it was Bakhtiar. Virginia, however, faced a tough schedule, including seventh-ranked Duke and ninth-ranked Army. After a surprising season-opening tie with powerful West Virginia, the Wahoos stood 1-2-1 heading into their October 19 meeting with Tech at the Tobacco Bowl in Richmond.

By 1957, Moseley had fielded three good teams in as many years. His 1957 squad, stocked from a great recruiting year in 1954, had the potential to be Tech's best ever. "We figured we had some good football players, people who wanted to play," recalled Mac McEver.

On the other hand, the athletic department's finances remained pinched. Money from the initial fund-raising surge of the early '50s had gone to stockpile talent for the teams. But fund-raising and finances were a constant battle. Though Tech had given between 15 and 20 scholarships each year through the 1950s, to compete with the powerhouses, it would have to ante up.

This situation showed Moseley that he needed to spend more time as athletic director. He hoped the 1957 team would be strong enough to allow him to steal that time from his coaching chores. Before the season, Moseley moved his office upstairs, out of the football offices, to concentrate on administration.

In retrospect, McEver said, "Maybe we thought those '57 seniors were better than they were."

Whatever happened, the 1957 Hokies disappointed early and were just 2-2 headed into the Virginia game.

Tech great Carroll Dale.

They were still favored. Another wrong call.

"Things began to look good for the Cavaliers right from the opening kickoff," *College Topics* reported. "Tech's Frank Eastman made the mistake of letting his knee touch the ground while picking up the ball, and Tech found themselves on their own one-yard line."

It never got any better for the Gobblers; Bakhtiar made sure of that. He rushed for 158 yards and four touchdowns. By game's end, he had scored 26 points, including placements kicked. Bakhtiar even pulled a third-quarter quick kick out of the dust bin, and it was good for 57 yards. Tech helped the Wahoo cause, fumbling five times (losing four), throwing five interceptions, and having a punt blocked. The victory-hungry Cavs romped over the Hokies 38-7.

Moseley gritted his teeth afterward and told reporters, "We got the hell beat out of us."

"It was a sight to warm the heart of the most jaded Virginia fan," *College Topics* trumpeted on Monday. "Our Prince picked up 153 yards and would have touched on the 200 mark but for a few penalties."

Bakhtiar's selection to the Football Writers All-American first team added some polish to what ultimately proved to be a disappointing year. Although the Cavs surprised Carolina in the last game of the season, they finished 3-6-1, which was enough to see Martin head out the door after just two campaigns. He was replaced by another young coach, Dick Voris, from San Jose State. Instead of getting better, things got very bad in a big hurry.

Voris's teams went 1-29 in three seasons, tying an NCAA record with 28 straight losses. The Hokies were only too happy to inflict their share of pain on the Wahoos during that stretch.

With Carroll Dale in his arsenal, and opposing defenses finding it easier to tighten up on his conservative offensive style, Moseley opened his attack in the 1958 season. He faced one major problem: he had only 14 lettermen returning. Tech managed a lackluster 5-4-1 campaign and gained notoriety for starting 155-pound Dick Rinker at fullback.

A visit by Miss America Mary Ann Mobley highlighted that year's showdown in Roanoke. Though mired in a season of losses, the Cavs managed somehow to keep it close. Tech's Billy Holsclaw threw for two touchdowns and ran for another in a 22-13 win.

"I remember that Reece Whitley, our quarterback, was leading the nation in total offense coming into the game," recalled Virginia's Sonny Randle, who went on to play as a receiver for the St. Louis Cardinals. "He hurt his knee, and that was pretty much it for the year. More than anything, I remember a one-handed catch I made in the end zone. I still have the picture in my scrapbook."

By the 1959 season, Tech's coaches found themselves with an experienced line; only Holsclaw, their stellar quarterback, was lost to graduation. Carroll Dale turned in his usual exceptional performance his senior year, and Alger Pugh, who later would become an excellent high school coach in Danville, lived up to his billing as a strong runner. Averaging 5.5 yards per carry, he rushed for 615 yards and eleven touchdowns, enough to earn him a spot on the All-Conference team with Dale.

The Hokies finished 6-4 while the Cavs gave up 403 points in 10 straight losses. "Disgusting," *College Topics* said after a 37-0 loss to William and Mary to open the season. The Cavs at least scored against Tech, before losing 40-14 in Richmond.

Moseley's last team, 1960, was another solid club that should have won the Southern Conference championship. Instead, in a late season mental lapse, the Hokies were upset by Davidson and George Washington to finish 6-4. The Wahoos, meanwhile, suffered through another 0-10 record. "When will it end?" the *Cavalier Daily* (*College Topics* renamed) asked in mid-October, just days before Virginia endured another thrashing, 40-6, in Roanoke. "It was a really sickening show," the campus newspaper said afterward.

Tech's Terry Strock took the opening kickoff 89 yards for a score, and minutes later the Hokies drove for another touchdown. Then two minutes later, Tech's Tommy Watkins returned a punt 72 yards to

make it 19-0. The pattern was all too familiar to the Wahoo faithful. Their team would give up points in bunches, then settle in meekly to ride out another rout.

The Cavs were so bad that other ACC schools talked about evicting them from the conference. Clemson coach Frank Howard began openly calling Cavalier players "white meat." In its six years in the conference, Virginia had won four games and lost 24. Tech, meanwhile, was campaigning for ACC membership. But, having to deal with one weak team from the Old Dominion, the Carolina schools weren't about to risk adding another.

The Cavs closed out the season with a 28-0 loss to South Carolina for, appropriately enough, their twenty-eighth straight defeat, tying the record for most losses set by Kansas State from 1945-1948.

"It's time for another change," the *Cavalier Daily* said.

To many Wahoos, that sounded like a euphemism for keeping things the same.

Ned McDonald coached Virginia from 1953-55, during which he compiled a record of 5-23, including three losses to the Hokies.

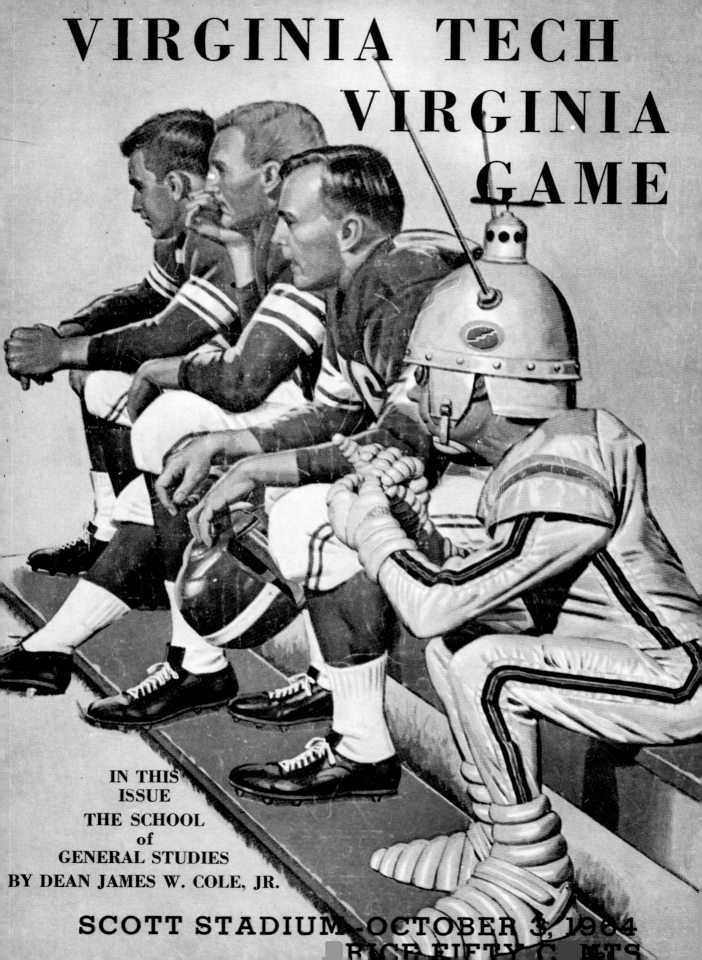

VIRGINIA TECH

VIRGINIA GAME

IN THIS
ISSUE
THE SCHOOL
of
GENERAL STUDIES
BY DEAN JAMES W. COLE, JR.

SCOTT STADIUM · OCTOBER 3, 1964

PRICE FIFTY CENTS

THE SIXTY-SOMETHING SIMMER

"On the grounds of the University, where the BULK cult grows daily, the question is simply, 'To BULK or not to BULK,' and almost everyone is BULKING."

—*Cavalier Daily*, September 1963

Both Tech and Virginia went hunting for a new coach in 1961. The Hokies found someone to see them through the whole noisy decade. And the Wahoos? Well, they got a bit closer to finding an athletic identity suitable for the school, but they still continued to drift in that netherworld of mediocrity.

It should be pointed out that the decade wasn't easy for either school's program. The Fighting Gobblers continued their search for a home in the ACC, and the Cavs sifted through several more personalities looking for one that fit.

Tech officials didn't have to look far for a new coach. They went to Bear Bryant's braintrust of bright young assistants and selected Jerry Claiborne, who had played on Bryant's teams at Kentucky in the late 1940s. Frank Moseley was an assistant coach at

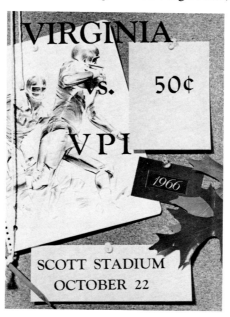

The 1966 Harvest Bowl game program. *Opposite:* The Cavaliers defeated the Hokies 20-17 in a 1964 thriller.

Kentucky then, and was familiar with his abilities.

As a player, Claiborne had shown tremendous determination, overcoming a lack of athletic talent. He wasn't big or fast, but he exuded desire and hard work. He started at offensive end and safety for the Wildcats. By 1949, his last season, he was voted the team's Most Valuable Senior.

Upon graduation form Kentucky in 1950, he coached at Augusta Military Academy, then in 1952 became a Bryant assistant at Kentucky. He followed Bryant to Texas A & M when the Bear moved there in 1954. As Bryant's defensive coach, Claiborne transformed the Aggies into one of the top defenses in the nation. Bryant's 1956 team won the Southwest Conference championship, ranked eighth in the nation in total defense.

The next season, Frank Broyles brought Claiborne to Missouri as his defensive coach, and there

Claiborne put together a pass defense that ranked second nationally. Then he did the same for Bryant at Alabama in 1958 and 1959, when the Tide led the nation in pass defense.

As a defensive coach for the top college teams in the nation, Claiborne's star had risen swiftly. Perhaps that was why he hesitated in January 1961 when VPI athletic officials began making overtures to him. He was also more than a little loyal to Bryant. In fact, Claiborne probably wouldn't have gone to Blacksburg if it hadn't been for the Bear.

"Go on up there and give those fellas a football team," Bryant told his assistant.

On January 16, Claiborne and his wife flew into Roanoke, where Moseley met them. The next day he was interviewed, and the Tech people liked him so much they didn't see the

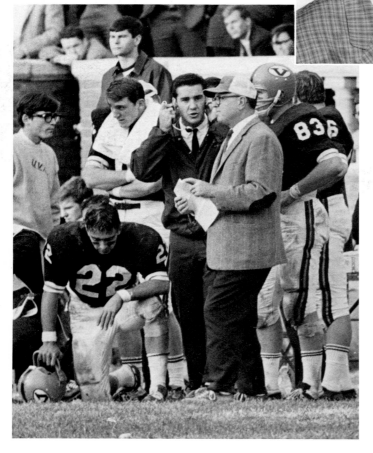

George Blackburn took over the the reins at Virginia in 1965.

need to look further. The following Saturday morning, January 21, the athletic council phoned Claiborne and offered him the job. He accepted, giving the Fighting Gobblers a reason to crow.

Virginia's coaching choice was another young one, but this time it worked or at least came close. Bill Elias, thirty-six, a native of Martin's Ferry, Ohio, had played as a quarterback three years at Maryland. His first coaching job had been in Richmond, Indiana, where he produced a pair of undefeated teams. That snared him a spot as a defensive backfield coach at Purdue for seven seasons. Then, in 1960, George Washington lured him away. As head coach, he rapidly turned their program around, driving the Colonials to a 5-3-1 record and himself into Southern Conference Coach-of-the-Year honors in one short season.

More important, his team had whupped Tech, 21-8.

That was good enough for the Wahoos.

"We expect to move the ball," he said upon taking the job.

That they would, though there remained a few indignities for the Wahoos to suffer.

"We have more to go on than just hopes that prospects for an early recovery at Virginia are good," he said after spring training. "The physical appearance of this year's squad impressed us when we first arrived in Charlottesville in January, and there has been a noticeable return of confidence."

The 1961 Cavs beat William and Mary, 21-6, their first time out, putting to rest the fear that they would set the record for all-time futility with 29 straight losses. Their elation was short-lived, however; the very next week they suffered a 42-0 drubbing against Duke, and then lost to North Carolina State. There the slide stopped; they beat VMI to head into their October showdown with

Tech sporting a 2-2 record. It almost seemed like old times.

Just like all new head coaches, Claiborne had jumped on the recruiting trail right after he arrived in Blacksburg in 1961. Topping his list of signings was a swift young quarterback named Bob Schweickert from Midlothian High outside of Richmond. The 1961 crop also included running backs Sonny Utz, Dick Kelly, and Darrell Page, and hard-hitting linemen Burton Mack Rodgers, Vic Kreiter, Lynn Jones, and Mike Hvozdovic.

Within two years, Utz and Schweickert would develop into solid offensive threats, the explosive elements in a sound Tech attack.

For the most part, Claiborne built on a nucleus of good sophomores he inherited from Moseley—Jake Adams, Tommy Marvin, and Kyle Albright at ends; Gene Breen, Alex Camaioni, Newt Green, Dave Green, Jim Hickam, Larry Philpot, and Ron Frank in the line; Tommy Hawkins, Tommy Walker, Buddy Weihe, Lacy Edwards, Pete Cartwright, Mike Cahill, and Phil Cary in the backfield. Dickie Cranwell, younger brother of Bill and Bob Cranwell, developed into a fine placekicker.

Claiborne retained a trio of Moseley men—Bill Conde, Dick Redding and Jack Prater—as assistants, making the coaching transition smoother. To that group he added Hootie Ingram, the tough All-Southeastern safety who had starred for Bear Bryant at Alabama.

Moseley's toughness had mellowed over the years, and perhaps the underclassmen weren't quite prepared in 1961 for the hard-nosed Claiborne out of the Kentucky hills.

Tommy Hodges throws the game winning TD pass to Larry Molinari in UVa's 20-17 victory in 1964.

Larry Molinari catches the game winning pass from Hodges in 1964.

The Cavaliers celebrate the dramatic 1964 victory.

He was a devout Christian who demanded discipline. He had been accustomed to building defensive unity in his previous teams and made it clear he expected the same at Tech.

Schweickert learned of Claiborne's discipline the hard way. As a quarterback on the freshman team, he arrived two minutes late for an afternoon meeting in the fall of 1961 and spent the dusk after practice running long, hard sprints to the tune of Claiborne's whistle.

Although Moseley's last team was stocked with seniors, Claiborne had experienced quarterback Warren Price and running back Terry Strock to boost things for him in 1961. All in all, the coaches and fans expected a good season. In one respect it was. The Hokies beat Virginia, again.

The Cavs fumbled twice in the first quarter, leading to two Hokie scores. Then Tech's Terry Strock returned the second-half kickoff 96 yards for a touchdown, the same trick he had turned against the Wahoos the previous year. Warren Price threw two touchdown passes for the Gobblers on the way to a 20-0 win.

"They wanted to win; we didn't," the Wahoos' Elias said dejectedly afterward, adding that the game "was the most upsetting loss of my short head-coaching career."

His Cavs would finish the season 4-6, and while that was nowhere near what he wanted, it was as close to respectability as the Wahoos had been in three years. Meanwhile, Claiborne's first team finished 4-5, and the faithful weren't happy. The Blacksburg campus was growing and changing daily, losing its small

Above: After scoring with 4:50 left in the game, the Virginia defense stiffened to preserve the victory.

Below left: The Virginia victory in 1964 snapped a six-game losing streak to the Hokies.

Below right: Carroll Jarvis attempts to leap over Virginia Tech's line in the 1964 game.

military school identity and settling in for a period of substantial growth that would lead Tech to match the University of Virginia as a large civilian school.

The Hokie boosters reasoned that a technically oriented land grant university should have a big-time football program. They liked Claiborne's defense right off the bat, but his conservative approach to offense annoyed them. The Hokies wanted some excitement.

The 1962 season was beset by problems from the very start. Claiborne had a painful ruptured disc operation in early September as the team prepared to open the season. And Schweickert, a major figure in the coaches' backfield plans, suffered a shoulder injury, splitting the socket, just before the first game. He missed most of the first six contests, shortening what would become a brilliant college career to only 24 games.

The Hokies had already lost two games by the time they played Virginia on October 6. The Cavaliers were 1-0 after beating William and Mary to open Elias' second season, and they were sporting a new attitude. "Last year, we weren't sure what the coaches could do," said co-captain Carl Kuhn. "They've given the guys a feeling that we are in big-time football, and that we mean to compete in big-time football."

"We've proven to ourselves that we can win," agreed Cuozzo.

The Tech series, *Cavalier Daily* noted, was tied at 21 games apiece and four ties over the years. Virginia's last win was a distant memory. "Since 1953, the Gobblers have whipped Virginia eight out of nine times," the student paper added. "What mastery do the Techmen hold over the Wahoos?"

There was no answer to that mystery in 1962. The Cavs started out nicely, with Cuozzo leading them to a first-quarter drive, which he finished with a 10-yard run. Up 7-0, the game turned sour for the 'Hoos with a series of fumbles. Tech's Gerald Bobbitte scored from

the one in the second period, but the conversion failed, leaving Virginia up 7-6. After intermission, Bobbitte ran in another touchdown, and Claiborne's offense executed a two-point conversion for a 14-7 lead. Phil Cary scored in the third for a 20-7 Tech advantage, but Terry Sieg returned a punt 79 yards to pull Virginia to 20-15 with a two-point conversion.

Virginia got the ball back for a late drive, and Cuozzo pushed the Wahoos down to Tech's six-yard line with one minute left to play. The Cavalier fans in Victory Stadium ached for a big play. But it was the same old story. In the final, heart-stopping seconds, somebody fumbled—and Tech recovered.

"The Cavaliers have once again fallen under the spell," *Cavalier Daily* lamented on Monday. The student newspaper explained that, for years, the Wahoos had competed with the belief that they were the superior team, but with the recent victory, Tech had edged ahead in the series, its first lead.

This truth notwithstanding, the Wahoo ticket office did a brisk business that next fall as fans sensed that Elias was about to herd the team into winning territory. Such optimism quickly dissipated with a pair of losses to Duke and Carolina opening the 'Hoos schedule. Suddenly, the season seemed to hinge on the third game with the Hokies, again at Victory Stadium.

The Gobblers had lost at Kentucky, then whipped Wake Forest. Still, good feelings abounded in Blacksburg. Tech insiders jokingly called the 1963 group Claiborne's "Ragamuffin Team"—not many superstars, just solid, dedicated players. "Claiborne got

Tech controlled the 1966 game.

more out of that team than any I ever saw," Mac McEver said.

Bob Schweickert agreed: "I would do anything for that man. That's the kind of team we had. We played for the coach. We had such a belief in Jerry, we'd go into a game believing we could win, even if the odds were heavily against us."

The backbone of the team was again Claiborne's brilliantly coached defense. The offense was Schweickert and Utz, "Mr. Inside and Mr. Outside." As with the quarterback, Utz had developed as a sophomore, revealing the value he would have as a

Defensive lineman John Naponick (79) trips a Tech running back in the 1966 contest.

blocker and inside runner, preventing the defenses from keying too heavily on Schweickert.

"He's the reason I had the success I did," Schweickert said of Utz, a 5-foot-11, 208 pounder from Annandale. "He was very unselfish, one of the best blocking backs in the country. Without Mr. Inside to keep those guys close, Mr. Outside would not have had nearly the success he did."

As he had every summer, Schweickert, in those months before the 1963 season, worked on the weak element in his game—passing. He wasn't a poor passer, just erratic. His frustration swelled on seeing an open receiver and not getting the ball to him.

Through the summer and into fall practice, he threw 300 to 400 passes a day; the maximum number thrown by pro quarterbacks only runs from 120 to 150. The pace wreaked havoc on the tendons in his arm, sending intense pain running from his first finger to his elbow. At times, blinding pain would prevent him from lifting his arm to take a snap from center. It would be a pain he would take with him to the New York Jets and on into his adult life as a businessman.

Despite the pain, he kept working. "Schweickert was the type of athlete who kept getting better," McEver said. "He worked hard all the time. He didn't even walk between classes. He ran."

Wisely, Claiborne built the offense to the team's strength: Schweickert's open-field running and Utz's line bucking. The passing game featured only sprint-outs and options. There was no drop back throwing, no post patterns, no large passing gains. Still, Schweickert's work paid off, giving the Gobblers a third threat to go with Mr. Inside and Mr. Outside. Passing on the option, Schweickert would complete 62 of 116 attempts for 687 yards that season. He would rush for another 839 yards (then a conference record on 155 carries, a 5.4-yard average). His total offense for the season, 1,526 yards, was also a conference record.

As good as all of that sounded, little of it would be a factor in the 1963 meeting with Virginia. Instead, Tech's defense would make most of the difference. The Hokies scored early, then just before the half ended, Dickie Cranwell set a Tech field goal record with a 40-yarder for a 10-0 lead. Claiborne's defense took care of the rest, and the Wahoos found themselves with yet another loss.

Down 0-3 on the season, the Cavs struggled to finish 2-7-1, deflated. In the aftermath, Elias revamped his staff, bringing back former head coach Ned McDonald to coach the line and offensive-minded George Blackburn to help find some punch.

The Hokies, meanwhile, finished 8-2, including wins over Florida State and West Virginia. The result was their first outright Southern Conference championship—also their last, as they left in search of bigger things.

Bob Davis runs for daylight in his attempt to avoid the Hokie defense.

For the first time in school history, the Gobblers had four players named to the All-Conference first team—Schweickert, Utz, Gene Breen, and Newt Green. Tommy Marvin was voted to the second team. Schweickert and Claiborne were named the conference player and coach of the year, and Schweickert was selected third-team All-American by the Associated Press. As a result, Jerry Claiborne was awarded a new five-year contract, extending his original four-year agreement.

Gary Cuozzo quarterbacked the Cavaliers from 1960-62.

Sixteen seniors graduated from Claiborne's championship squad. In 1964, he replaced them with highly skilled sophomores: Sands Woody, Andy Bowling, Richard Mollo, Ron McGuigan, and Erick Johnson in the line, and Tommy Groom in the backfield.

Though he reworked his offensive and defensive lines, the Tech coach still fielded the same attack—Utz up the middle and Schweickert running the sprint out, run-pass option. Schweickert sustained an injury early in the first game against Tampa, leaving Utz to carry the offense. The fullback delivered with 31 carries for 146 yards and two touchdowns. Cranwell added a 29-yard field goal. It was enough for an 18-14 win.

The 1964 Hokies were a young team. It would, in fact, develop into one of Tech's best, although the record would reflect a couple of tough early-season lessons. The toughest lesson was taught by the Wahoos.

That year, the game left Roanoke and returned to Charlottesville.

Elias installed a weight-lifting program for his team in the spring of 1963, and when his players went home for the summer, he followed them with a note-writing campaign

Hokie quarterback Bob Schweickert had his collegiate career cut short by a shoulder injury.

to remind them to keep lifting.

When they returned to campus in August, the results were impressive. Tackle Bob Kowalkowski had put on 35 pounds of muscle, weighing in at 265.

"The right side of the University of Virginia's offensive line probably will be the largest in college football this year," wrote Virginia sports publicist Gene Corrigan (who would go on to become ACC commissioner) in *Cavalier Daily*. His piece touted the cult of "bulk" that the weight-lifting program had brought to the team. Besides Kowalkowski, there was guard Ted Torok at 245 and end Don Parker at 265.

The real deal, though, was the Cavs' new "pro" offense, featuring a variety of rollout option plays to take advantage of Virginia's talented quarterbacks, Tom Hodges, Bob Davis, and Stan Kemp.

Of the three, the six-foot, two-inch, 200-pound Davis, a sophomore, had the biggest upside. His scrambling had charged the spring alumni game.

"He's an exciting, colorful quarterback, who in the alumni game displayed a knack for continually getting himself in trouble, but finding a way out," *Cavalier Daily* reported. "On one third down play, for example, he was trapped fifty yards behind the line of scrimmage only to throw a sixty-yard strike for the first down."

Despite these new additions and high hopes, the Wahoos lost their first two games of the 1964 season and were winless heading into the Tech game in Charlottesville. "The fans at Virginia are tired of listening to excuses," *Cavalier Daily* offered the day before the game. "There is only one thing that Wahoos rooters will accept tomorrow, and that is victory. Nothing else will suffice."

The Hokies scored just enough to put the Cavs in a hole, and Virginia trailed 17-14 with 1:21 to play and the ball on their own twenty-one-yard line. Here, the tide turned. First, Bob Davis connected with Roger Davis, who turned a screen pass into a twenty-three-yard gain. Then Davis hit John Pincavage with a pass, and he ran to Tech's forty-two.

Tech stalled things there by batting, and almost intercepting, a Tom Hodges pass. So Blackburn called for the screen again, from Davis to Davis, and the Wahoos carried the ball to Tech's twenty-nine with just thirty-three seconds left. The Hokies rushed hard on the next play, but Hodges ducked away and found Larry Molinari just as he broke open in the secondary for the winning touchdown.

Sonny Utz, in a 1986 newspaper interview, recalled the anger in Claiborne's eyes that day. "It was a long ol' bus trip back to Blacksburg," he said. The trip was followed by a brutal practice on Monday.

"I'd never seen him as mad," Utz said of his coach. "That may have been the loss that upset him the most."

Utz, however, retained one other memory of that day. "I remember their big ol' guard. Kowalkowski.

I got bent over backwards and started hollerin' for people to get off me. He jumped in the pile and started throwin' guys every way until I got out. I might have been hurt if it wasn't for him doing that."

The Wahoos rode the momentum of the big finish to a 5-5 record, and, figuring that breaking even was the best he could do, Elias left for the head-coaching job at Navy after the season, leaving Blackburn to run the program.

Tech closed out a disappointing 5-4 year and the college careers of Utz and Schweickert with a big win over VMI.

If the day marked the passing of two Tech stars, it also heralded the arrival of another. Sophomore running back Tommy Francisco scored Tech's last touchdown on a 57-yard pass reception that displayed his savvy for broken-field running. Francisco came to Tech a dancing, shifty runner from Southwest Virginia, but he left as one of the greatest power backs in school history.

That April, VPI announced it would withdraw from the Southern Conference at the end to the school term. The move, recommended by the board of directors of the Athletic Association, was approved by the

Below left: Bob Schweickert talks to a teammate.

Below middle: Frank Loria was one of the Hokies' most feared, and aggressive, defensive players. (Photo Virginia Tech Information)

Below right: George Foussekis was an integral part of Tech's dominating defense in 1966. The Hokies defeated UVa 24-7 that year although Foussekis was ejected early in the game .

Above: UVa coach Bill Elias with QB Gary Cuozzo and tackle Dave Graham. (Photo UVa Sports Information)

Right: UVa coach Bill Elias. (Photo UVa Sports Info)

university's Board of Visitors. In announcing the change, new president, T. Marshall Hahn explained that Tech wanted to keep its relationship with conference schools, but it also wanted to schedule schools with larger athletic programs. What Hahn didn't say was that Tech still held out hope for admission to the Atlantic Coast Conference.

The spring game that year indicated that Tech might just be ready. Claiborne had a grand defensive chemistry cooking, with sophomores George Foussekis and Dan Mooney at ends, Clarence Culpepper at linebacker, and Jeff Haynes and Don Thacker at tackles. The veteran leaders were Billy Edwards at linebacker, and Mike Saunders, at guard.

Claiborne had his strongest weapons in the defensive backfield, where sophomores Frank Loria and Wayne Rash were showing an affinity for racking up tackles. On offense, Claiborne made use of other fine sophomores: ends Gene Fisher and Ken Barefoot, and running back Dickie Longerbeam. And to replace Cranwell, Claiborne had found an English soccer kicker, sophomore Jon Utin.

With Schweickert's graduation, Bobby Owens emerged to set a school record for the most accurate passing season that next fall. In leading the 1965 Gobblers, he completed 68 of 122 passes, a .557 percentage. That and solid defense gave the Hokies another fine 7-3 record.

Against Virginia, Longerbeam rushed for 164 yards in 28 carries to lead the Hokies, 22-14. The game marked the official dedication of Lane Stadium. Tech had celebrated the opening of Miles Stadium 40 years earlier with a victory over the Wahoos, and the Hokies were tickled to repeat the trick in initiating Lane.

It was Homecoming, and the crowd exceeded

Due to the temporary stoppage of the series, Frank Beamer only participated in one Virginia game as a player. (Photo Virginia Tech Sports Information)

30,000. The corps of cadets, now overwhelmed by the "civilian" student body, performed its usual white hat trick in the stands, spelling out BEAT UVA.

The Hokies had certainly done that often enough to feel good about their land-grant heritage.

Tech's 1966 team was packed with talent, and even without a passing game, the Hokies showed a multifaceted ground attack in Tommy Francisco, Ed Bulheller, and Dickie Longerbeam. But Tech was shut out by Tulane in the opening game, 13-0 and Longerbeam shattered several cervical vertebra, putting an early end to what could have been a brilliant season.

The Hokies marched on without him, adding three wins and a tie with West Virginia before drubbing the Wahoos 24-7 in Scott Stadium. Tommy Francisco scored three touchdowns, and the defense held Bob Davis to just 74 yards total offense. It proved to be a momentary setback for the future pro. He would go on to lead the ACC in offense in 1966 and was honored as the Conference Player of the Year. Another young Cavalier back that day, Frank Quayle, would earn the same honor in 1968.

But Virginia had had enough of the Hokies for a while. The Cavs had decided not to reschedule Tech until 1971, leaving another break in the 51-game series.

Perhaps it was for the best. The Wahoos were headed for more losing while the Hokies were going bowling. They finished 8-2-1 in 1966 and earned an invitation to meet Miami in the Liberty Bowl.

Their biggest defensive star that year was junior safety Frank Loria, the greatest and saddest of Tech football stories.

Coming out of Clarksburg, West Virginia, Loria

was overlooked by the pride of his home state, West Virginia University, because he lacked speed and size. He didn't fit the formula for a major college prospect. But his four years of play for Tech proved something to West Virginia and other colleges about their recruiting philosophies: their formulas couldn't gauge that undefined essence of a real football player. Loria had the instincts, the fearlessness, and above all, the inner defensive urge, a nearly insatiable need to put the big chill on a ball carrier.

Loria was a quiet, even-mannered, polite kid off the field. On the field, he reeked of meanness, a combination of instinct and simple physics. Only 5-foot-9, 175 pounds, he showed an unteachable knack for knowing where he should be and propelling his small body to that spot with astounding momentum.

For years, Mac McEver had a hand in coaching the Tech defensive backs. He'd tell them to hit the receiver hard on every play. "They wondered why you'd try to take the fellow's head off," McEver recalled. "I'd tell them, 'You just hit him every time he comes through the line. You take the crack at him because that's the guy who's going to be running at you in the fourth period. You want him tired. You want him leg weary. You want him to know he's gonna get the hell knocked out of him. He'll be thinking about all those things, and then maybe that'll win the game for us in the fourth quarter.'"

It was Loria's nature to deliver that same kind of punishment—without having to be reminded. "Loria, I was his fan," McEver said. "He won as many games for us as anybody on defense. I told [assistant coach]

Alf Satterfield the first year Loria played, 'You ought to award him two letters—one for linebacker, one for safety.'"

Loria's style was the spearhead of one of the most vicious defenses in Tech history—the 1966 unit. John Raible, George Foussekis, and Mooney were ends; Sal Garcia, Clarence Culpepper, and Ken Whitley linebackers; Dave Farmer, Sands Woody, Jeff Haynes, Andy Bowling, Don Thacker, and Waddey Harvey on the line; Ron Davidson, Jimmy Richards, and Frank Beamer in the backfield.

"That defense hurt people," said Ken Barefoot, a

Johnny Watkins and Terry Strock were named MVPs in the Hokies' 40-6 victory in 1960.

Tech offensive end who went on to a career with the Redskins. "We used to hate to scrimmage against them in practice."

Claiborne's practices were matters of attrition. By design, only the tough survived. "We went to war every single day," Barefoot said. "The physical stress was tremendous. Butting drills, circle drills, board drills—that's the way they coached.

"But the coaches left Loria alone because he always knew what he was doing. He had the instincts."

Those instincts would make him Tech's first consensus, All-American. In 1966, the season of the Hokies' first of two trips to the Liberty Bowl, he was tabbed for the Associated Press and Football Writers Association first teams and Helms Foundation second team. For 1967, his senior season, he was selected to the top seven first teams—AP, UPI, NEA, American Football Coaches Association, Football Writers, *The New York Daily News*, and the Walter Camp Football Foundation. Along with Barefoot, he played in the East-West Shrine game as a senior.

In the 31 varsity games Loria played at Tech, he returned 61 punts for 813 yards and four touchdowns. He intercepted seven passes. He guided an excellent class of players to 22 wins, seven losses, and one tie. But his real talent, his incredible capacity for hitting, couldn't be measured, except perhaps in the groans of opponents.

To that style he added solid academic achievement and exemplary personal habits, which earned him academic All-American honors two years running.

"He was somewhat shy," Barefoot said. "He didn't relish all the publicity the All-American status brought him. I think he tolerated it."

Despite his accomplishments in four years of college, Loria was passed over in the professional draft. "I think it really, really hurt him badly," said Barefoot, who was drafted by the Redskins in the fifth round that year. Loria signed a free-agent contract with Denver Broncos but didn't make the team's regular roster.

After some graduate work at West Virginia University, he joined the coaching staff at Marshall in 1969, working under head coach Rick Tolley, a Tech linebacker from 1959-1960. Loria, Tolley, and their Marshall team were among the 75 fatalities when a Southern Airways DC-9 crashed just short of the runway at the Huntington airport on November 14, 1970. The news of the tragedy shook the entire Tech community.

"No other athlete has brought as much recognition and honor to the university during his playing days as

The Hokies thrashed UVa 20-0 in 1961. (Photo VT Special Collections)

did Frank Loria," Claiborne said in eulogy.

Loria's spirit typified the ideal that both schools had struggled to find over the years, that perfect balance between athlete and scholar. Neither school could seem to reach a comfortable solution to the conflicts that arise between academics and athletics. With the growing commercialization of college sports, finding the answer to that dilemma would become increasingly difficult. The lines of definition seemed to blur with each passing season.

One thing, however, did remain clear for Virginia and Virginia Tech. There, among the heavy questions, was the usual fun, the spirit of that old rivalry, that old Virginia class warfare.

Bluebloods vs. bumpkins.

'Hoos 'n' Hokies.

The stereotypes aren't accurate, of course. But the one-upmanship is real.

"These Agriculturalists may have played like farmers," *College Topics* observed after the first game between the two schools in 1895, "but they have bravely gotten over it."

Maybe. And only maybe.

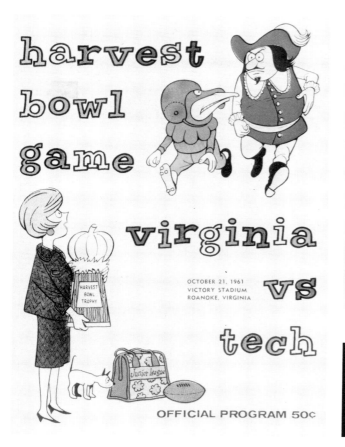

Only the Hokies reaped benefits of the 1960 Harvest Bowl. (Photo VT Special Collections)

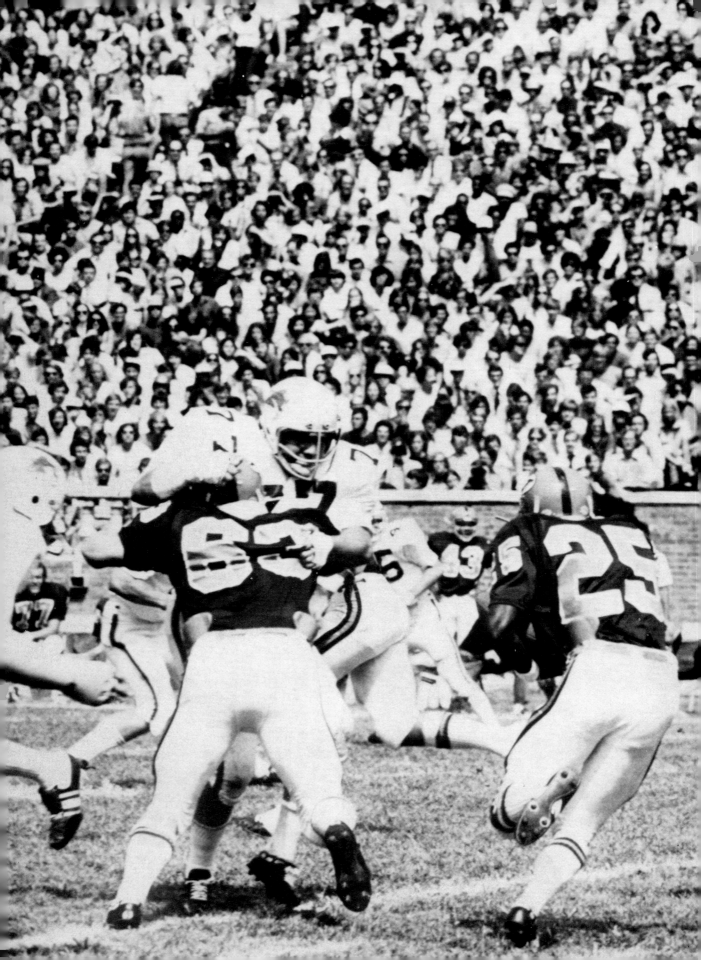

PART II - BIG TIMES

BY DOUG DOUGHTY

OFFICIAL PROGRAM
ONE DOLLAR
NOVEMBER 6, 1971

'71

VIRGINIA
vs.
VIRGINIA TECH

SCOTT STADIUM
CHARLOTTESVILLE,

OPENINGS WEEKEND

THE COLLEGE GAME

THE RESUMPTION

"If you can't get excited for Tech week, they better put you to rest. And, I'll feel the same way when they're putting me in the box."

—Sonny Randle, Virginia player (1956-1958) and head coach (1974-1975)

The series was halted in 1966, with the only provision for a resumption being one game in 1971. The Cavaliers claimed they wanted to concentrate on conference games, but there were suspicions Virginia no longer felt it could compete after losing 12 of 14 games between 1953 and 1966.

Clearly, the two football programs had a different mission. Athletic director Frank Moseley, the Hokies' coach from 1951-1960, had hoped Tech would achieve national prominence when he hired 32-year-old Jerry Claiborne as his successor. The Hokies had moved into 40,000-seat Lane Stadium for the 1965 season, while Virginia played and continues to

Virginia coach Sonny Randle stalks the sideline.

play at Scott Stadium, which did not undergo significant renovations until the mid-1970s. There was reason to question the commitment of the entire Atlantic Coast Conference, which required a minimum score of 800 on the Scholastic Aptitude Test. A court challenge by two Clemson swimmers put an end to the "800 Rule," but not before South Carolina dropped out of the ACC and the conference nearly broke up in 1971.

There were years in the 1960s when Tech brought in as many as 50 scholarship players and Virginia as few as 20, but the series wasn't as lopsided as the cessation of play might have indicated. Virginia beat the Hokies 20-17 in 1964 in Charlottesville—only the

Right: Sonny Randle was 5-17 during his two years with the Cavaliers.

Below: Sonny Randle barks instructions during a time-out.

Below middle: Sonny Randle leaves the field after a 24-17 loss to Tech in 1975.

Below right: Despite his struggles, one of Sonny Randle's five career victories was a 28-27 decision against the Hokies in 1974.

Virginia guard Tom Glassic (79) and quarterback Scott Gardner await action against the Hokies in the 1975 game.

second time since the 1940s that the game had been played at a campus site—and then fell 22-14 the next year in Blacksburg. Tech beat the Cavaliers 24-7 in 1966 in a game that was noteworthy, many years later, as the first start for a Hokies' sophomore from Hillsville: 5-foot-9½ defensive back Frank Beamer. Beamer would see the Cavaliers again—when he was named Tech's head coach in 1987.

The Best Game Never Played occurred—or didn't occur—in 1968. The Hokies won their last five games to finish 7-3, the same record posted by a Virginia team that set ACC records for scoring and total offense. In a conference in which no team had ever gained more than 400 yards per game, UVa averaged 439.4.

The Hokies received their second Liberty Bowl bid in three years, but Virginia stayed home and went without a bid to postseason play until 1986. UVa was the last major college football team to play in a bowl, but that piece of trivia is misleading. The Cavaliers were under consideration in 1986 until it was learned that five UVa starters were graduate students, including record-setting quarterback Gene Arnette and All-ACC offensive tackle Greg Shelly. The rule has since been changed, but graduate students were not eligible for postseason play at the time.

The Tech-UVa series was revived in a meeting at the Howard Johnson's motel atop Afton Mountain, the gateway between the eastern and western parts of the state. Bill Matthews says he and Tech athletic director Frank O. Moseley had been lobbying Virginia athletic director Steve Sebo for several years without regard for time or place—at national conventions, golf outings, wherever they saw him. Matthews, a former Hokies' basketball star, was Moseley's long-time assistant.

"Steve Sebo was the man, who, through all the years, we've given credit for getting it started again," Matthews says. "Steve was never against the series. He went over the objections of his coaches. I think we actually met three years before we started again and it had to fit the schedules, which is why we later ended up playing [in Charlottesville] two years in a row. They weren't drawing flies and Steve could see what a gate it could bring. We promised to bring 10,000 people; then, when we played two or three years later, they wouldn't let us have the tickets. The first game [in 1970] was the first time we went over $100,000 in payoffs for both teams."

Sebo, then nearing retirement age, was succeeded as athletic director by Gene Corrigan, who says there was still some scattered opposition to playing Virginia Tech when he took office January 1, 1971, though by then the series had been resumed, with the teams scheduled to play in 1971, and 1973 through 1980. Moseley was eager to play the Wahoos in 1972, and, at a Charlottesville Quarterback Club luncheon, he offered Sebo a guarantee of $70,000 if the Cavaliers would come to Lane Stadium that year. "You can have the $70,000 even if we don't make a dime," Moseley said.

Inset: Tom Fadden catches a pass in the 1974 game.

Tailback Joe Sroba busts through the line in 1974.

At the same luncheon, two days before the 1970 game, then-UVa coach George Blackburn reported that somebody had broken into the Cavaliers' locker room the previous night. Nothing was taken, but when Blackburn entered the locker room the next morning, he was greeted by two turkeys perched atop a pair of shoulder pads. There were turkey droppings all over the floor, a story since verified by former assistant athletic director Jim West. "You [Blackburn] did it yourself," charged Moseley in mock dismay. "You'd do anything to win that football game. That should get your team psyched up."

Although the story sounds authentic, Virginia already had all the motivation it could get after a 1969 season in which it was shut out four times and lost its last six games. The Hokies, who had gone 4-0-1 over the last five weeks of the 1969 season, were the home team and were expected to win by 30 points; however, Tech ticket manager, Tom McNeer, was concerned about the turnout. Tickets were going for $7, the highest price ever charged for a football game in Virginia, and as this was the opening game, some students had not yet returned to school.

A crowd of 23,000 watched the Cavaliers hold Tech to 201 yards and hand the Hokies their first shutout loss, 7-0, since 1962. UVa defensive tackle Andy Selfridge was applauded by Claiborne and by longtime UVa assistant Ned McDonald. McDonald proclaimed he had never seen a better performance by a defensive tackle. "We never did hear that $40,000 scoreboard of theirs," said UVa wide receiver Bob Bischoff in a telling statement about the Hokies' big-time aspirations at the time.

The Virginia Pep Band taunts the Tech faithful.

Left: The Cavaliers celebrate their controversial 28-27 victory in 1974.

Right: Frank Block, a third-year medical student at the time, directs a parody of "'Ole McDonald Had a Farm" to goad the Hokies.

Below: The famed Virginia Pep Band performs at halftime.

Scott Gardner attempts to avoid the Hokie pass rush.

Scott Gardner fires a pass down the field.

The Tech mascot watches action on the Scott Stadium field.

The 1970 UVa game was the beginning of the end for Claiborne, or at least the beginning of a season-opening five-game losing streak, the Hokies' second in as many years. Two days after Tech's loss to South Carolina, bringing its record to 0-4, word leaked out of a meeting between Moseley, school president T. Marshall Hahn, and Claiborne. Claiborne was officially out as coach at the end of the season.

While many felt the program had grown stagnant under Claiborne, others questioned the way Claiborne was handled. Tech officials, however, noted an erosion of support—financial and otherwise—that did not improve when the Hokies won five of their last six games.

Roscoe Coles scores a touchdown in 1976 at the same spot on the field where Bruce Arians was stopped in 1974. (Photo VT Special Collections)

Only 7,000 were in the stands at Victory Stadium in Roanoke when Tech ended the season with a 20-14 win over VMI. Claiborne, the winningest football coach in Tech history, had an overall record of 61-39-2.

Within four days of the Tech-VMI game, Claiborne and Keydets' coach Vito Ragazzo were dismissed. Virginia coach George Blackburn hung on a little longer. The Cavaliers finished 5-6—only one UVa team since 1952 had won more games—but lost all six of their ACC games as their

Mike Bennett scampers 64 yards with a kickoff, but was stopped short of the endzone.

conference losing streak rose to 10 games. Blackburn was summoned to a meeting with Corrigan and Vice President of Student Affairs D. Alan Williams, ostensibly to review the season. He was told his contract would not be renewed. Before the end of the meeting, a news release had been delivered to the *Richmond Times-Dispatch*. By the time Blackburn arrived home, his wife and family already had heard the news on television.

"The shot already had been fired and I was dead," Blackburn says. "My wife greeted me at the door with tears in her eyes. They're [Corrigan and Williams] digging pretty low. When they look in the mirror to shave in the morning, they better take a good look at themselves."

Claiborne had the advantage of six weeks' notice to prepare for his dismissal, but he took a few parting shots, apparently intended at the meddlesome Hahn and Hokies boosters. "I have always received 100-percent cooperation from Frank Moseley," Claiborne said in a statement. "We have been and continue to be proud of the program we have built together.

"While I personally believe that success is measured by more important considerations—some perhaps intangible—I cannot help pointing with pride to the school's first and only conference championshp, the participation in two major bowl games [and] the appearances of our team on national television. Surely, no 'disgruntled' critic—official or unofficial—can deny that these honors focussed more widespread national recognition on our university than at any other time."

Hindsight says maybe Virginia and Tech were too hasty in replacing their head coaches. Claiborne, who had rejected an overture from Baylor two years earlier, took a job as an assistant at Colorado and in 1972 was named head coach at Maryland. He took over a Terrapins' program that had gone 9-42 over the previous five seasons and compiled a 10-year mark of 72-37-3, including ten victories in ten games against Virginia, five of them shutouts.

History has been kind to Claiborne, who compiled a 179-122-8 record in 28 seasons as a Division I head coach, the last eight at Kentucky, his alma mater. He wasn't the most exciting of coaches, either in personality or style of play, but his teams were fundamentally sound. More important, they won. Claiborne-coached teams were invited to 11 bowl games and his Maryland teams of the mid-1970s won 23 consecutive games against ACC opponents, a record until Florida State joined the conference and began to dominate the football race in the 1990s.

Unlike Claiborne, 42 when he left Tech, Blackburn was 57 and already near the end of his coaching career. Blackburn, whose 1968 UVa team had set 19 ACC records, would not get another college job, but his offensive expertise made him valuable to several NFL teams as a scout. He had a .500 record as late as midseason of his sixth year

The Cavalier mascot at the 1972 Virginia Tech game.

Harrison Davis, one of the first black players at UVa, lines up during the 1973 game.

Harrison Davis (15) hands off to Kent Merritt (25) in a 24-20 Virginia victory in 1972.

at UVa, and his overall record of 29-32 would have been the envy of several of his successors.

Gene Corrigan, not officially athletic director but very much in control, decided that a younger man would be needed to take Virginia to the next level, though by elevating 34-year-old defensive coordinator Don Lawrence to the head job, he acknowledged that not all was wrong with the Blackburn regime. Lawrence, well-respected, was not the least bit colorful or controversial. Taking its usual opposite tack, Tech went looking for a promoter when it began its search for a successor to Claiborne.

It was reported that LSU coach Charlie McClendon would be offered a then-unheard of package of $500,000. Those rumors eventually died down, and speculation centered on a couple of young firebrands: Arkansas defensive coordinator Charlie Coffey and Louisville head coach Lee Corso. President Hahn, who made no secret of his ambitions for Tech's football team, took an active role in the selection process and handpicked the 36-year-old Coffey, whose aspirations were no less grandiose than Hahn's.

It is convenient to trace the "modern era" of Tech-UVa football to 1970 because that is when the series resumed, but, more important, it was then that the black athlete first had an impact at both schools. Tech signed its first black football player to a scholarship in 1968—fullback John Dobbins from Radford. Virginia

Left: Fans look for a respite from the sweltering heat in September of 1972.

Right: The 'Hoos mascot stands in front of the Virginia Tech cheerleaders.

Inset: UVa co-captain Tom Kennedy shakes hands with an unidentified Hokie prior to the start of the game in 1972.

Dave Strock has a field goal attempt blocked by Stanley Land (99), but the Hokies would prevail 6-0 in the 1971 contest.

QB Mitcheal Jones looks to pick up first down.
(Virginia Tech Sports Information)

signed four black players in the winter of 1970—Harrison Davis, Kent Merritt, Stanley Land, and John Rainey—although these players did not suit up in a varsity game until the fall of 1971. (Freshman eligibility for football and basketball did not begin until the following year).

Roanoke Times columnist Bill Cate was to write that Claiborne's lack of success in recruiting the black athlete might have led to his downfall, but in the context of Claiborne's entire career, it would be wrong to suggest that he was unwilling to recruit black athletes. It was a transitional period for many universities and college football programs and Tech was not the only school that moved slowly in recruiting black athletes or was viewed with some skepticism by potential black students. The same could be said of Virginia.

Although integration of both programs clearly was under way by 1971, Tech's first black player of note—and a Claiborne recruit, no less—was running back James "J.B." Barber from Charlotte, North Carolina, who was the leading rusher for a Hokies' team that took a 2-5 record into Scott Stadium that year. The Hokies had lost their first four games, but had scored

39, 41, 37, and 27 points in succeeding weeks and boasted the nation's total-offense leader in previously forgotten junior quarterback Don Strock.

A crowd of 30,100—the largest at Scott Stadium in nineteen years—saw the Cavaliers contain Don Strock but lose 6-0 on a pair of field goals by Dave Strock, Don's older brother. The real heroes, however, were on a previously undistinguished Tech defense that stopped the Cavaliers five times inside the Hokies' 24-yard line. Virginia outgained Tech 318-248, but was victimized when placekicker Billy Maxwell missed on field goal attempts from 30 and 22 yards, the second of which was blocked.

It was an odd twist for the resumed Tech-UVa series: the second consecutive shutout victory by a road team not known for its defense. Tech was to give up 56 points the next week at Houston, a team that Coffey feared, but not enough to tone down the rhetoric as he left Scott Stadium. "I have trouble going to sleep every night thinking about two things," says Coffey, a notorious workaholic who may have been one of college football's first burnout sufferers. "I worry about the next team we have to play and I can't sleep. And, I'm so elated about our future, I can't sleep either. . . . It was a damn important win to us."

Coffey's offensive coordinator and the man who resurrected Don Strock's career was Dan Henning, a former William and Mary quarterback who was an assistant for the Washington Redskins during their glory days and later served as head coach of both the Atlanta Falcons and the San Diego Chargers. Indeed, Henning crossed paths with the Hokies again in the mid-1990s, when he returned to the college ranks as the head coach of Big East Conference rival Boston College.

Strock's return prompted Coffey to hype the upcoming season as "Explosion '72," a slogan that had dud potential with Virginia waiting in the opener. The Cavaliers found something even more enticing than Frank Moseley's $70,000 guarantee two years earlier at the Charlottesville Quarterback Club: the Hokies not only agreed to come to Scott Stadium for the second year in a row, but the Cavaliers had the advantage of having played a game, a 24-16 upset of South Carolina in Columbia.

That was quickly forgotten by the UVa fans, who

tency and eventually had to move to wide receiver, a position he later played in the NFL with the San Diego Chargers. On this day, however, Davis shrugged off a sore shoulder suffered in the South Carolina game and helped the Cavaliers score 24 unanswered points and win 24-20 before an overflow crowd of 31,300—the third largest in the school's history.

While Virginia failed to capitalize on its 2-0 start, the first since 1954, the Hokies overcame an 0-2 start to finish 6-4-1, their first winning record since the Liberty Bowl season of 1968. Hopes were high for Year 3 of the Coffey regime, but neither sophomore Ricky Popp nor freshman Eddie Joyce, Jr., could meet Strock's standards at quarterback, and when the Hokies entertained Virginia on October 20, 1973, they stood at 0-6. Disenchantment with Coffey was brewing.

Tech's offensive staff stifled its pass-happy instincts and tried to win the game on the ground. J.B. Barber, by now a senior, rushed for 116 yards in the first half and finished with 138 yards on 21 carries. Sophomore Phil Rogers added 136 yards on 24 carries, but it was Doug Thacker, a 186-pound sophomore defensive end, who was instrumental in the Hokies' 27-15 win. Thacker had two sacks and two fumble recoveries, the second with the score 17-15 and the Cavaliers in Tech territory.

"How does 1-6 sound?" Coffey was asked after the game. "A hell of a lot better than 0-7," was his predictable reply. "It wasn't the Super Bowl and it's obvious we're not going to any bowl games. But, I can't imagine anything feeling better. It's been a long time coming."

There was speculation as early as mid-October that Virginia would change coaches and the move, predictably enough, came two days after a 42-17 loss at West Virginia. That dropped the Cavaliers to 4-7 for the season and 11-22 in three seasons under Lawrence, who said he left the program "in 200-percent better shape" than he found it, but otherwise was not embittered. "If Don Lawrence is not rehired, it is because we have lost for 20 years," Corrigan had

Opposite above: **As a sophomore Phil Rogers gained 136 yards against UVa in a 24-20 loss in 1972.** (Photo Virginia Tech Sports Information)

Opposite below: **The debate still rages about whether or not Ricky Scales was in-bounds when he made this TD reception in the Hokies 28-27 loss in 1974.** (Photo Virginia Tech Sports Information)

Opposite: **Don Strock on the sidelines.** (Photo Virginia Tech Sports Information)

Above: **J.B. Barber gained 116 yards against UVa in the first half in 1972. He finished the game with 138 yards on 21 carries.** (Photo Virginia Tech Sports Information)

started to boo Harrison Davis when Tech took a 14-0 lead late in the first half. As if it weren't burden enough to be a black quarterback in the school's first class of black football players, Davis was plagued by inconsis-

Above: Don Strock (15) holds the ball for his brother Dave (46) in the Hokies' 6-0 victory in 1971.

Left: Doug Thacker returns an interception against the Cavaliers in the Hokies' 24-17 victory in 1975. (Photo Virginia Tech Sports Information)

Below left: Rick Razzano puts the clamps on a UVa ball carrier in 1975. (Photo Virginia Tech Sports Information)

Below right: Bill Houseright (73) deposits a UVa quarterback on the turf. (Photo Cary Shelton)

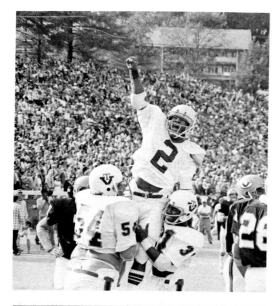

said late in the season, "not because he had lost for three."

Roanoke columnist Bill Cate was among those calling for Coffey's resignation following a 22-21 season-ending loss to VMI. "Coffey, undoubtedly, is a great promoter," he wrote. "He is a great organizer. But this isn't a side show. This isn't the ferris wheel. So, you fill the seats. So, you sell the players on your school. The next step is to get them to play for you. Charlie Coffey hasn't done that. . . . Coffey motivated the alumni to give tickets and give money. But, he has not motivated those with whom he has had day-to-day contact."

The executioner never came, however. Coffey regretfully replaced defensive coordinator and close friend George McKinney with South Carolina aide Billy Clay. Hahn left town on a trip to the South Pole and Coffey disappeared briefly from the sports pages, to be replaced by Ulmo Shannon "Sonny" Randle, introduced December 5, 1973, as Virginia's new coach. Randle had played for the Cavaliers, leading the ACC in receptions in 1958, before suiting up for five different teams in the NFL. An applicant for the Virginia job following the 1970 season, Randle had put up a 22-10 record in his three seasons as the head coach at East Carolina.

In his introductory news conference, Randle didn't wait long to make reference to Coffey, who had a helicopter at his disposal for recruiting. "We don't have a helicopter here," Randle said, "but we do have some fast airplanes. You'll see my smoke." Coffey had too many worries to be bothered by Randle. The word in Blacksburg wasn't good. Recruiting wasn't going well, and Clay stunned Coffey with his resignation; he returned to South Carolina three weeks after taking the Tech job, amid speculation that he hadn't been able to attract the kind of defensive coaches he wanted.

Still, there was little indication of the change that was about to take place. Coffey decided some time in the evening January 3, 1974, that he would resign; he flew out of Roanoke by private plane the next morning. "I decided several years ago that I would coach until I was 40," says Coffey, who was 39 at the time. "After the dismal flop of the [1973] season, I decided to coach one more year, [but] after more thought, it wouldn't be fair to bring in new staff members, knowing I was only going to coach one more year."

It was barely 1974, and Tech and UVa were both preparing to welcome their third different coaching staff of the decade. The Hokies thought they would be looking for a new athletic director—possibly Coffey—after Moseley announced December 5, 1973, that he would retire at the end of the school year. But, the search for an athletic director was put on hold while Tech went about the business of hiring a new football coach. As it turned out, Moseley was to remain four more years.

Tom Beasley forced this fumble to preserve a 24-17 Hokie victory in 1975. (Photo Virginia Tech Sports Information)

Unlike the Coffey hire, which was a Hahn production, Moseley had a big say in the 1974 search and was committed to "finding a football coach and not a salesman." He remained true to his Bear Bryant ties and hired Jimmy Sharpe, Alabama's 34-year-old offensive coordinator, who had called plays in the Crimson Tide's 833-yard, 77-6 rout of the Hokies the previous season. Sharpe, a former 187-pound Crimson Tide linebacker, was handsome and personable and was well-liked by his players until the final days of his tenure. He brought with him the Wishbone, an option offense that was all the rage at the time, but later became obsolete because it lacked catch-up capabilities.

For the Wishbone to be effective, the team needed a quarterback who could read a defense, fake, run when needed, and pass in an emergency. Sharpe didn't have many quarterbacks on his roster and he certainly didn't have any option quarterbacks. The Hokies' only quarterback with any eligibility was Bruce Arians, who was so unhappy with the way things had gone under Coffey that he had decided not to return if he could find a job coaching in junior high school.

"[Assistant] Terry Don Phillips talked me into coming and meeting Jimmy Sharpe," recalls Arians, now an assistant at Mississippi State after a stint as the head coach at Temple. "Jimmy said, 'Come on out for spring and, if you can't make it, I'll get you a high-school job.' I said, 'Shoot, I've got nothing to lose but twenty pounds.' I went back in after two weeks and asked, 'What's the deal?' He said, 'You're the captain of the team. You're the starting quarterback. You'll start all eleven games unless you break a leg.' It was a dream come true for me.'"

A rians had never played in a Tech-UVa game until his fifth year, 1974. He had entered fall camp in 1973 as the starter, but did not start the opening game. He regained the No. 1 job for the second game, but after the Hokies returned from Southern Methodist University in the fourth week, he dropped from starter to scout-team quarterback. When Tech entertained Virginia on October 20 that year, Arians was sitting in the stands at Lane Stadium at what he now considers the low point of his career.

It was no wonder, with his career resurrected under Sharpe, that Arians viewed the 1974 UVa game as "the biggest game of my life. . . . I don't know anybody who goes there; I just don't like the school." The Hokies had opened with four straight losses in Sharpe's inaugural season, but were coming off a 31-17 victory over two-touchdown favorite South Carolina. Like Tech, Virginia was 1-4, but showing signs of progress under Randle, witness a 22-21 loss the previous week to eleventh-ranked North Carolina State.

A crowd of 32,149 watched junior quarterback Scott Gardner throw a pair of fourth-quarter touchdown passes to enable Virginia to overcome a 14-7 deficit and take a seemingly insurmountable 28-14 lead in the fourth quarter. The Hokies had not completed a pass in nine quarters—not that they had attempted many—before Arians connected with Ricky Scales on a 24-yarder that set up a 1-yard Arians touchdown plunge with 7:44 remaining. Then, with no time remaining, Tech cut the deficit to 28-27 on an 11-yard pass from Arians to Scales.

The Cavaliers protested that Scales had a foot out of bounds, but that was nothing compared to the uproar

Coach Jerry Claiborne and John Dobbins, the first black football player at Virginia Tech.
(Photo Virginia Tech Sports Information)

that resulted from the two-point play. The call was an "option right," with Arians following a block by fullback George Heath. In the eyes of many Hokies' faithful, Arians crossed the plane of the goal, but there was no signal from the officials. They huddled briefly, but didn't change the call as the Cavaliers celebrated and the Hokies mourned. "There was a pretty good fight, as I recall," Arians said.

"It's still a very vivid memory for me," he continued. "If we had made it, the memory probably would have faded away, but it's like it happened yesterday. I was lying in the end zone, my waist was on the goal-line, and all around me I could hear my teammates cheering. Then, everything went crazy. I never got an explanation, which was the most furstrating thing. There was one guy I knew from high school, Brian McDevitt, who's a lawyer now in Philadelphia. He always tells me, 'We knew you scored, but Scales was out of the end zone.' "

Rick Razzano crunches a UVa ball carrier in 1975.
(Photo VT Special Collections)

The 1974 loss stuck with Tech fans, making their 24-17 victory in 1975 all the sweeter. (Photo VT Sports Information)

Phil Rogers in 1975 action against UVa.
(Photo UVa Special Collections)

Sharpe, who had an endearing quality, met Randle at midfield after the game and told him, "Sonny, if they let us stay around long enough, you'll have to have a lot bigger place to play." Sharpe was right about one thing: Virginia put decks on both sides of Scott Stadium that would push the permanent seating to 40,000. But Sharpe and Randle weren't around to see it. Neither was coaching football in Virginia when he turned 40.

There is no more compelling story in the UVa coaching annals than Sonny Randle's. Randle dreamed of taking his alma mater to football prominence and saw that dream shattered in two quick seasons. To Randle's credit, he has not faded into oblivion, even after a short-lived coaching comeback at Marshall. He has served as a commentator on Marshall games and is a sports director for several radio stations in Virginia. The Sonny Randle Sports Minute is heard all over the state.

Randle, with all his passion, could not handle losing. He was able to deal with a 4-7 record in 1974, when progress was obvious, but his emotional tirades in 1975 only served to divide the team and make a bad

situation worse. The Cavaliers gave up 60 or more points on three occasions during a 1-10 season, although the situation didn't really begin to deteriorate until after an October 18 meeting with Tech.

The 1974 game will be remembered for the most controversial finish of the Tech-UVa series in recent years, but it was one of several close games. In 1975, Tech entered the game with a three-game winning streak and roared to a 21-6 halftime lead at Lane Stadium, but Gardner, who was to finish his career owning all of UVa's passing records, led another comeback that had the Cavaliers trailing 21-17 as they began their final

Buddy Weihe recovers a Stan Fischer fumble.

drive. On first-and-10 from the Tech 14, however, Gardner was blindsided by Tom Beasley, who caused a fumble that was recovered by Mike Stollings with 49 seconds left.

That helped make up for some of the disappointment of 1974, but redemption wasn't complete until the Hokies returned to Scott Stadium in 1976. Arians, by now a Sharpe assistant, had gone out before the game and placed two strips of adhesive tape in the end zone where the two-point play had been foiled two years earlier. "Only four people knew they were there," Arians said at the time. "And, if one of them hadn't touched it, I wouldn't have told a soul." Arians could tell his story because, with 1:08 remaining, Tech running back Roscoe Coles ran over the same spot on a 1-yard touchdown run that gave the Hokies a 14-10 victory.

In the process, they kept Virginia winless—at 0-6—under first-year coach Dick Bestwick. Bestwick, a long-time Virginia Tech assistant, had been a finalist in 1973 when Virginia hired Randle. When it all ended too quickly after the disastrous 1975 season, the only finger-pointing Randle did was at himself. "I don't think Virginia was ready for Sonny Randle, and I'm not sure Sonny Randle was ready for Virginia," he said recently. "I had experienced a lot of success [at East Carolina] and the losing just tore me up."

Bowie

Of the seven games he coached against Virginia Tech, the one that stands out in Dick Bestwick's memory was the first. Bestwick remembers little of the circumstances of the game—a 14-10 defeat that extended the nation's longest Division I losing streak to fifteen games—but he remembers the consequences.

"Probably the most poignant thing I remember about the Virginia-Virginia Tech series is Kevin Bowie lost his life after that [1976] game," recalls Bestwick, later the athletic director at South Carolina and now an athletic administrator at Georgia. "And it was in a way that was particularly appalling to me. The one thing I never taught was spearing [tackling with the helmet]. Matter of fact, I did the exact opposite.

"Kevin, who was a great kid and a good player, came in and speared that big fullback they had [Paul Adams] and hit him in the buttocks. Kevin jammed his neck real bad and couldn't practice the next week. We didn't take injured players with us on trips, so he came to see me in the middle of the next week and asked if he could go see his grandparents in Washington, D.C. I said, 'Yeah, that'd be fine, Kevin. Just take care of yourself.'"

The next week, Virginia snapped the long losing streak on a spectacular, late-game touchdown reception by Andre Grier, who was Bowie's roommate. No sooner did the Cavaliers enter the locker room, however, than they were told by Bestwick that Bowie had been murdered the previous night at a Washington-area McDonald's.

Dick Bestwick sends instructions in the game.

STATE OF FLUX

"I have a lot of respect for the [Virginia] football program, the school, the Jeffersonian atmosphere. But, there's something about the preppiness that wasn't really for me."

—Mickey Fitzgerald, Virginia Tech tight end and fullback (1975-1978)

From the time it left the Southern Conference following the 1964 season until it joined the Big East in 1991, Virginia Tech was an independent in football. The Hokies' basketball teams and non-revenue teams were affiliated with the Metro Conference and, starting in 1995, the Atlantic 10. However, it has long been Tech's goal to belong to an all-sports conference, and while Jerry Claiborne is not clear on many of the details from his 300-game coaching career, he remembers the Hokies casting an eye toward the Atlantic Coast Conference as early as the mid-1960s.

This enthusiasm was one-sided. Despite repeated overtures, the only time Tech actually came to a vote was in 1977, when the Hokies received sponsorship from Virginia, Clemson, and Duke. A committee visited Blacksburg, and Tech made a presentation to the seven member schools, volunteering to accept reduced shares of television and bowl revenues until at least 1980. ACC representatives met May 2, 1977,

Dick Bestwick was 2-3-1 against the Hokies.

at Research Triangle Park between Raleigh and Durham, North Carolina, but needed only thirty minutes to reject expansion. From most indications, Tech did not come close to the five votes it needed for acceptance.

"The special meeting is a kind of hoax in itself," wrote columnist Art Chansky of the *Durham Sun*. "The Virginia Tech question has been hanging for so long that, in effect, three ACC schools sponsored the Hokies as much to get the issue resolved as anything else. At least one of the schools, Duke, is expected to vote against letting Tech in. . . . Schools that cherish their allotment of ACC tourney tickets, and the income the tickets generate from donators (sic), aren't going to give them up for dear old Virginia Tech."

What made the situation particularly galling for the Hokies, however, was the ACC's decision in 1979 to admit Georgia Tech as an eighth member. That was followed, 12 years later, by the acceptance of Florida State. In truth, ACC tournament tickets had little to do with Tech's rejection. At the heart of the rejection were the twin issues of geography and TV exposure. Georgia Tech allegedly brought the ACC into the Atlanta television market. Florida State gave the ACC an entry into Florida for recruiting and television purposes. What Virginia Tech offered was competitive teams and facilities, but little from a marketing standpoint.

"I wouldn't say we were downhearted," said Frank Moseley, who was to remain Tech's athletic director for four years after his first proposed retirement in 1973, "but I would say we were disappointed. I've read that this was the second time we've applied, but this is the first time to my knowledge. We didn't actually apply this time. The ACC has no method for applying. We had three sponsors and I think they consider the fact that we were interested as being an applicant. But, I don't ever remember a formal application."

Bestwick consoles a player after a tough loss.

A 6-5 record in 1976 gave Tech back-to-back winning seasons for the first time since 1967-1968, but there were some cracks in the Sharpe foundation. Defensive coordinator Charley Pell was hired away by Clemson following the 1975 season, under what many considered a coach-in-waiting situation. When Pell was named to succeed Red Parker as head coach following the 1976 season, he came after Tech offensive line coach Danny Ford, who shared Sharpe's and Pell's Alabama connection. Moseley reportedly gave Sharpe carte blanche to hire the best two assistants he could find, but an intensely loyal Sharpe elevated graduate assistants Bruce Arians and Mike Yeager.

In the end, however, the demise of the Sharpe era could be traced to a meeting of the Roanoke Valley Sports Club, which each August brought together the head coaches of the state's "Big Five" football programs (Tech, UVa, VMI, William and Mary, and Richmond). By the time he addressed the group, Sharpe apparently had become intoxicated, a development that was not met with great tolerance by Tech officials. William Lavery, who by then had succeeded T. Marshall Hahn as Tech's president, gave thought to firing Sharpe immediately but was convinced that a coaching change less than a month before the season would plunge the program into total disarray.

"Refresh my memory," asks Mickey Fitzgerald, a tight end and fullback who was Tech's most celebrated signee of the Sharpe Era. "I knew from recruiting that [Sharpe] liked to have a drink. They all do. But, I never thought it affected his dealing with the team. Another thing you have to remember: Bob Vorhies died in practice that year. My backup, Bob Vorhies. I haven't

Bestwick in practice.

Left: Don Lawrence talks with Kent Merritt (25) and Harrison Davis (15).

Right: Don Lawrence coached the Cavaliers to a 24-20 upset of the Hokies in 1972.

experienced much in my life that was as catastrophic. A kid dies following a workout—a 18-year-old, good-looking kid who was the national shot put champion, scholastically gifted—and you see everything fall apart. If there was ever any question [about Sharpe] before, that did it. If the Salem thing was the beginning of the end, that was the end."

It was the hope of Sharpe's supporters that if the Hokies had had a successful 1977 season and their man could have avoided any more embarrassing incidents, the Sports Club affair—not reported until months later—would have been forgotten. Instead, there was only growing disillusionment as the Hokies lost their first three games. Tech was only 1-3 after a 31-8 victory over William and Mary, but the Hokies were favored by 20 points for an October 15 meeting with Virginia at Lane Stadium. Not only had the Cavaliers lost their first five games, but they had been shut out four times in the process, including a 68-0 drubbing by Texas that stands as UVa's worst loss since 1890.

Second-year coach Dick Bestwick, realizing that the situation couldn't get any worse, bypassed starting quarterback Bryan Shumock and backup Ted Manly in favor of Chip Mark, who had not played in a varsity game during his three-year UVa career. Indeed, one week earlier Mark had been the quarterback of record when the Cavaliers' junior varsity had lost to VMI 13-0. All three quarterbacks worked with the first unit during practice, but Mark didn't learn that he would start until 30 minutes before game time—a decision that Bestwick had made privately earlier in the week.

Mark completed 10 of 17 passes and had the Cavaliers on top 14-3 before he was sidelined following a numbing hit by Tech defensive tackle Danny Hill. A career-long 56-yard field goal by Paul "Chile Bean" Engle, so named because he was raised in Serena, Chile, pulled the Hokies to 14-6 with 7½ minutes left. But it still took a 70-yard touchdown drive and a two-point pass from David Lamie to Kenny Lewis in the final 45 seconds for Tech to knot the score at 14. It is the only tie in 45 Tech-UVa games since 1946.

Victories over Wake Forest and VMI in the final two regular-season games weren't enough to save Sharpe, who was fired with four years remaining on a contract that paid $31,210 per season. There were reports that Lavery told Sharpe he "did not fit the image" of the university, but it was clear that the Hokies had not been headed in the desired direction after an 8-3 season that put Tech on the brink of a Tangerine Bowl bid in 1975. The staff, which once had included three future Division I head coaches in Pell, Ford, and Nelson Stokley (Southwestern Lousiana) had clearly slipped. And the Wishbone offense, starting to put up some numbers with former tight end Fitzgerald at fullback, just lacked excitement.

Only one day after Sharpe was fired, Moseley, who had been at Tech since 1951, announced his retirement. At 66, it was certain that he meant to leave. With Tech in need of both an athletic director and a football coach, Lavery made it clear that he would not be hiring the coach. "I think the selection of the coach is the athletic director's job," said Lavery, adding that he had no intention of hiring an athletic director who

Above background: UVa defeated the Hokies 20-18 in 1979.

Above: Billy Harris breaks into the open field.

Right: Steve Potter tackles Cyrus Lawrence in 1979 action.

Background: Superman drops in on the 1977 game, but neither team proved to be heroic in the 14-14 tie.

Inset: Cavalier defensive tackle Ron Mattes attempts to break up a pass. (Photo Dan Grogan)

would also serve as football coach.

North Carolina coach Bill Dooley visited Blacksburg on January 3, 1978, prompting speculation that he was in town to lobby for Clyde Walker, a former Carolina football assistant and then the athletic director at Kansas. Walker and one-time Duke athletic director Carl James, executive director of the Sugar Bowl, were considered the leading candidates for the athletic director's job. The media had less to say about a prospective coach, though names like head coaches Charley Pell from Clemson, Fran Curci from Louisville, and Bobby Bowden from Florida State had surfaced.

The Hokies generally had taken another program's top assistant—Jerry Claiborne, Charlie Coffey,

Sharpe—so there was little to suggest that they could get a head coach of Dooley's stature. Dooley was credited with building the North Carolina program, leading the Tar Heels to back-to-back ACC championships in 1971 and 1972, and rebuilding the program following the death of Carolina player Bill Arnold in practice. In 1977, the Tar Heels went 5-0-1 in the ACC, captured their third conference championship of the Dooley Era, and played in the Liberty Bowl.

Dooley had almost left Carolina one year earlier, however, tentatively accepting the head coaching position at Miami. He was at the airport when he changed his mind. "They had offered me a heckuva deal," says Dooley, currently the director of sports development for the state of North Carolina. "Pete Elliott was

Above left: Bryan Shumock picked up a fumble and ran 89 yards
for a TD in UVa's 20-18 victory in 1979.

Above right: Defensive tackle Brian Tomlin sacks Tech quarterback David Lamie.

Below left: Cavalier cheerleaders.

Below right: Charles McDaniel, who captained the 1985 UVa team, caused a furor
with his remarks about Bruce Smith.

Cavalier fullback Mark Sanford.
(Photo Michael Bailey)

Stuart Anderson (99), Jim Hyson (65) and Keith Lee (88) chase Tech QB Steve Casey.
(Photo Michael Bailey)

the athletic director there at the time. They offered more money and more fringe benefits [than Tech would], but they didn't have the AD position to offer.

"I wasn't going to Virginia Tech," Dooley, then 43, says. "They offered me the head coaching job and I thanked them and said I appreciated it. Then, they came back and offered me the AD and head coaching job. The day I accepted it, [Bill] Brill wrote a column—and he tried to prove it for nine years—that they never should have given both jobs to one person. He blasted everything. Well, if they hadn't done it, I wouldn't have been there. In retrospect, it might not have been a good thing, but I wanted to be my own boss.

"When Dr. Lavery said what his goals were and what he wanted to do, I was sold. They wanted to be competitive, they would like to get into a conference, they wanted to do what it took from a standpoint of facilities and financial support. He didn't say anything about national championships. Of course, I didn't expect all that. I think a lot of people were [shocked] that I would leave the University of North Caro-

lina. It [Tech] was a challenge to build another program. It was my decision. No one twisted my arm. They offered me one job and I said, 'No.' Then they offered me both jobs and I said, 'Yes.'"

The Hokies were upset by visiting Tulsa 35-33 in Dooley's debut, but had gotten back to .500 by their visit to Virginia in the seventh week of the 1978 season. Scott Stadium had an eerie look, its new upper deck unoccupied because of structural cracks. Nevertheless, a record crowd of 34,275 watched the Cavaliers give Bestwick his first victory in seven games against in-state opposition, outscoring the Hokies 17-7. Despite a broken thumb, quarterback David Lamie started and took Tech on a 96-yard touchdown drive on its first possession. After that, it was all Virginia.

One of Virginia's heroes was Chip Mark. Mark had finished the 1977 season as UVa's starting quarterback but was a victim of Bestwick's commitment to the Veer offense before the 1978 season. The backup to sophomore Mickey Spady, Mark was summoned in obvious passing situations. Ultimately, it was an injury to Spady that prompted Mark's

The scoreboard tells the tale as Hokie fans parade around Scott Stadium with the goal posts held aloft.
(Photo Brian Hoffman)

Above: Sean McCall returns a kick against the Hokies.

Right: Bryan Schumock, the hero in 1979, returns a kick.

Above: Greg Taylor is stopped in 1977 action.

Opposite: Tommy Vigorito goes over the top against the Hokies in 1978.

Dennis Womack has filled various roles since coming to Virginia in 1978. He is perhaps most recognizable as Virginia's baseball coach, though, as the Cavaliers' first compliance officer, he gave the rules interpretation in 1991 that led to an investigation of loans to student athletes. From the time he arrived in Charlottesville in 1978 until the mid 1980s, he was also the Cavaliers' athletic ticket manager.

It was UVa's practice then—and now—to make duplicate sets for those tickets that were sent to other schools. That way, if another school did not use its allotment, Virginia had the duplicate tickets on hand and could make them available to the public. In the case of the 1978 Virginia Tech game, Virginia knew that all seats in Section 101 would be purchased by Hokies' fans, which is why the spare set of tickets was locked in a vault in the UVa ticket office.

"I can't take all the blame," Womack says. "After all, I'd just gotten there. But, somehow, over th course of the fall [of 1978], the tickets mysteriousl got sold. The Virginia Tech people had gotten 101 and some Virginia people had got 101s, but we didn know it. Come game day, everybody's out in th parking lot socializing until about 20 minutes befor kickoff, when they start heading into the stadium. A of a sudden, we've got people looking at each othe and realizing they've got the same seats.

"Now, this place is packed. Not an extra seat in th house. If it's only two or three people, then, OK, n big deal. But, no, we've got hundreds of them. M supervisor on that side comes running to me and says 'Coach, we've got a counterfeiting problem.' I said 'What are you talking about?' He said, 'You won believe all those people over there in 101. They've a got the same seats.' I said, 'You're kidding me.' So I go over there and find out this is true. People fina

t I'm over there—the ticket manager—so they start llowing me around.

"There was a place over there where I could stand and finally I start trying to talk to these people who d been out in the parking lot and, I suspect, nsumed a few [refreshments]. But the one person o gave me the hardest time was a woman who must ve been 75 years old. She wanted to fight me. Her sband was the only one who would save me at that ne. She was a Virginia Tech fan and she was calling some names and told me, if I came off that platform, e was going to whup me. Of course, I wasn't about come down."

Womack got in touch with Ted Davenport, executive rector of the Virginia Student Aid Foundation, and s able to get his hands on a few extra tickets. Other ople were allowed to sit on a hill just outside the dium wall. "Still others got mad and left," Womack ys. "I went and told Mr. [Gene] Corrigan [the UVa

athletic director] in the fourth quarter and he really didn't think much about it. We were driving for the go-ahead touchdown at the time. But, at our Monday morning staff meeting, I brought it up again. I knew it wasn't going to go away and we already had started to get some calls: 'I want my money back.'

"Basically, what happened was, we gave their money back, but we still made money. The Virginia fans didn't want their money back; they were happy we won. We actually had a lot more people in the stadium than we normally have. But, we got some really bad publicity out of it. In the paper here in Charlottesville, there were letters every day for three weeks just ripping us. Sometimes my name was in there, sometimes it was just UVa: 'What are you all doing up there, you dummies?' It was a real mess."

entry in the fourth quarter against Tech. He led the Cavaliers on a late drive for an insurance touchdown, providing one more memory in a relationship with the Hokies that had started after the 1976 game.

"I was on my way back to my room," says Mark, a redshirt freshman at the time, "and I guess I had my name on my bag. A Trailways bus came by and somebody leaned out one of the windows and said, 'What do we have here? A sad Wahoo?' Well, I could have taken that, but then the guy threw his drink at me. Now, that was about as classy as a maroon leisure suit. So, I lunged at the bus and took a swing at him. But, then all the guys' friends threw their drinks on me.

Maurice Williams heads to the end zone for six of Tech's 48 points in 1983. (Photo Virginia Tech Sports Information)

Before it was all over, I'm not sure I didn't try to board the bus. . . . And, you have to ask why I love to beat Virginia Tech?"

T he most shocking result in UVa football history may have come in 1979, when the Cavaliers traveled to Georgia and routed the Bulldogs 31-0—one year before Georgia won the national championship. It definitely put a different spin on the UVa-Tech game the next week. All of a sudden, the Cavaliers found themselves with a 5-3 record and on the verge of their first winning season since 1968. UVa was an eight-point favorite, the first time in recent memory that the oddsmakers liked the Cavaliers over their in-state rival.

It was an odd situation in several respects. For one thing, through a scheduling quirk, Tech would be coming to Charlottesville for the second year in a row—the second time that had happened in the 1970s—with no apparent reward for the Hokies. Also, the game was to count in the ACC standings for

Jesse Penn returns an interception. (Photo Virginia Tech Sports Information)

a Virginia team that did not have a full conference slate, an ironic twist for the Hokies, who had been rejected for ACC membership only two years earlier.

The Hokies (4-5) had shown signs of promise in Dooley's second season, but they suffered a crushing blow one week before the Virginia game when senior fullback Mickey Fitzgerald suffered a season-ending knee injury in a 34-23 loss to West Virginia. Fitzgerald was not the ball-carrying threat in Dooley's I-formation that he had been in the Wishbone offense under Sharpe, but he was a punishing blocker for tailback Cyrus Lawrence, and a major presence in the locker room.

"I'd played 42 consecutive games at Tech, I've got a couple of all-star games I'm going to play in—that's sort of my consolation for not going to a bowl game—and I'm thinking I'm pretty indestructible," Fitzgerald says. "Next thing I know, I'm standing on the sideline on crutches [for the Virginia game] and the bowl game's disappeared, the all-star games have disappeared, and my market value is pretty questionable. At that time, the [surgical] procedure wasn't so good and I'd really blown it out bad. It was the height of being low."

As it turned out, Fitzgerald's absence was one of the main story lines, although it hardly seemed to matter when opportunistic Virginia took a 17-0 halftime lead. It had been 7-0, with Tech on the move late in the first quarter, when UVa linebacker Jim Hyson hit Lawrence. The ball popped into the waiting arms of Bryan Shumock, a one-time quarterback now starting in the secondary. Shumock's 89-yard touchdown return remains a school record.

At the start of the fourth quarter, with the score still 17-6, Tech quarterback Steve Casey connected with

Above: Gary Smith lets the world know that Cyrus Lawrence scored on the play. (Photo Virginia Tech Sports Information)

Above middle: Bruce Smith (78) and Ray Fitts (6) congratulate Bob Thomas on his interception return for a TD in 1984. (Photo Virginia Tech Sports Information)

Above right: Padro Phillips (76) celebrates a sack in the Hokies' 30-0 victory in 1980. (Photo Virginia Tech Sports Information)

Right: Vince Daniels flattens a UVa ball carrier. (Photo Virginia Tech Sports Information)

Far right: Tech coach Bill Dooley and Cyrus Lawrence. (Photo Gene Dalton)

Below right: James Robinson flew over the UVa offensive line for this 1983 sack. (Photo Virginia Tech Sports Information)

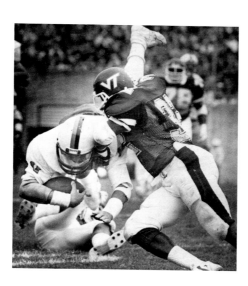

Above left: Dan McKillican (79) clears the way for Dan Hottowe (18) who nears the Tech end zone.

Above: Chip Mark spots the ball for Russ Henderson's field-goal attempt.

Above: Chip Mark (10) looks for running back Corwin Word (23) coming out of the backfield.

Right: Mickey Spady shouts out signals in Virginia's 17-7 victory in 1978.

Sidney Snell on a 25-yard touchdown pass. Tech tried for two points and failed, the first of three missed two-point tries. Late in the game, Tech scored on another Casey-to-Snell touchdown pass. With three seconds on the clock, Casey rolled out and spotted fullback Tony Blackmon in the end zone. Blackmon, a redshirt freshman starting in place of Fitzgerald, fell. The two-point pass was incomplete, and UVa prevailed 20-18.

Shumock argued that Blackmon fell because the ball was thrown behind him. Years later, the final two-point play does not stick out in Dooley's mind as much as the second try, when Casey was stopped with the score 17-12. "His whole body was in the end zone," says Dooley, bringing back memories of a similar call in Tech's 28-27 loss at Scott Stadium in 1974. "We got screwed, to put it mildly. We get that second two-point play and all we have to do is kick the extra point after the last touchdown and we win 21-20."

Snell's performance is not to be forgotten. A Blacksburg resident, Snell set a school record with 10 receptions, of which the most spectacular was a diving, one-handed catch on fourth-and-7 that kept the Hokies' final touchdown drive alive. The best the Hokies could have done at that point was a tie; Virginia freshman Wayne Morrison had kicked a 35-yard field goal that was deflected at the line of scrimmage, but fluttered over the crossbar with 5:33 remaining.

Virginia Tech was to win six of nine games with Virginia during the Dooley Era, including six of the last seven, but going into 1980, there was not a Hokies' player who had been on the field for a victory over the Cavaliers. Tech's 6-1 record that year was the Hokies' best after seven games since the 1967 team went 7-0, but skepticism remained because four of

Billy Harris scampers three yards for a score in the 1977 game that ended in a 14-14 tie.

the victories were over teams that subsequently would be classified Division I-AA—East Tennessee State, William and Mary, James Madison, and Rhode Island.

Success or failure in the Tech-UVa series often has hinged on injuries, or where the game falls in the teams' respective schedules. In 1980, Virginia was coming off a 27-24 loss to Clemson in what had to be the most painful setback of Bestwick's five-year tenure. The Cavaliers had never beaten Clemson—their 20-game series was the most lopsided in college football. UVa led the Tigers 24-10 to start the fourth quarter in Charlottesville, losing on a career-long 52-yard field goal by Obed Ariri with just six seconds on the clock.

The Cavaliers dropped to 2-3 for the season, easy targets for a Tech team that was getting progressively more irritated by the constant knocks against its schedule. "People talk about our schedule and they don't know what kind of team we have," quarterback Steve Casey said. "They haven't seen us and they didn't think we could beat Virginia. I've never seen a team that wanted to win a game so much. These guys could just taste it."

A Lane Stadium crowd of 52,000 watched in the

rain as Tech beat Virginia by the widest margin (30-0) since a 40-6 triumph over the Cavaliers in 1960. The conditions gave Dooley an excuse to run the ball even more than usual, with Cyrus Lawrence carrying 40 times—at the time a school record—for 194 yards and two touchdowns. The Hokies rushed for 295 yards as a team and had a 410-122 margin in total offense over a UVa team that did not penetrate the Tech 27-yard line. "It was the poorest game we've played in four-and-a-half years," Bestwick said, "[but] I'd attribute a lot of that to what Tech was doing."

One of the defining events of Bestwick's coaching career was taking place over the same weekend, though he didn't know it. Three days after the Tech-UVa game, Gene Corrigan announced that he would resign after ten years as the Cavaliers' athletic director to become the athletic director at Notre Dame. "If I said 'no' to this offer, I just wouldn't have been able to live with myself," says Corrigan, who had hired Bestwick and two other Virginia football coaches. "There's an old saying that the second son of an Irish family should become a priest. This [Notre Dame] is as close as I'll come."

Tech was rewarded for its 8-4 winning season in 1980 with a bid to the Peach Bowl. It was the Hokies' first bowl appearance since 1968 and their first winning season in four years. Clearly, Dooley had his program in place. It was the same formula he had used at North Carolina: a no-frills, ball-control offense; a strong kicking game; and a suffocating defense. Seven of eleven regular season opponents failed to score more than seven points against the Hokies in 1980.

The forecast for 1981 was looking bright. The Hokies won their first four games; however, the season took a downturn when Duke surprised Tech 14-7 in Durham, North Carolina. The most crushing blow came in the 10th week, when VMI had the last hurrah in its long rivalry with Tech and upset the Hokies 6-0. Dooley was so distraught that, for the first time in his Tech tenure, he called for a Sunday scrimmage. "After that [VMI] game, nobody could really believe we'd lost," Cyrus Lawrence said.

The Hokies were delighted that the Virginia game had been moved to the final week of the regular

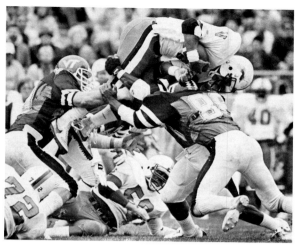

Left: Bruce Smith prepares to dump the quarterback. (Photo Virginia Tech Sports Information)

Above: Ashley Lee leads the charge as the Hokie defense stops a UVa running back at the line of scrimmage. (Photo Gene Dalton)

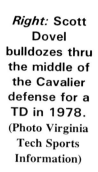

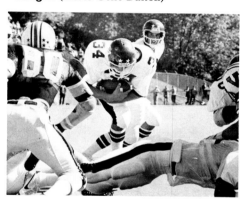

Right: Scott Dovel bulldozes thru the middle of the Cavalier defense for a TD in 1978. (Photo Virginia Tech Sports Information)

Above: Tech's Johnnie Edmonds waltzes into the end zone in 1980. (Photo Virginia Tech Sports Information)

season—the first time they occupied that spot in the history of the series. From 1913 through 1971, tradition held that Tech played VMI every Thanksgiving Day in Roanoke, but enthusiasm for that series waned during the late 1960s and the push for a Tech-UVa finale began almost as soon as the series resumed. Virginia ended its season against North Carolina every year from 1910-1950, after which Duke filled that slot for Carolina and the Cavaliers played an assortment of teams—most often Maryland—in the final game.

"When I first came here, Jimmy [Sharpe] and I talked about moving our game," Bestwick said. "That was when we were planning the addition to our stadium and it looked like we might install lights. I thought, if we wanted to have a big rivalry, we should play it when all big rivalries are played—either Thursday, Friday, or Saturday of Thanksgiving week. I told Mr. C. (Corrigan) and he apparently raised the issue with Bill Dooley."

Dooley favored meeting Virginia in the last game, but he preferred playing before Thanksgiving. There were weather concerns when the 1981 game was rescheduled for November 28—the original date was November 14—but a record crowd of 39,027 watched the Hokies put Virginia out of its season-long misery with a 20-3 victory. The Cavaliers lost starting tailback Malcom Pittman on the first series, and, lacking regular quarterback Gordie Whitehead, were intercepted four times.

If Tech had not stalled several times deep in UVa territory, it would have been a carbon copy of the 1980 game. Lawrence was unstoppable again, carrying 38 times for 202 yards in a fitting climax to a marvelous season. This performance enabled Lawrence to finish the season with 1,403 yards—still a Tech record. Against Virginia alone, he rushed for 494 yards in three games. A knee injury caused him to miss most of the 1982 game.

"He was a stallion before there were the Stallions," says Billy Hite, a Tech assistant who used that term to describe latter-day tailbacks Maurice Williams and Eddie Hunter. "Cyrus, at that point in time, was so much stronger than anybody else on the field. Physically stronger. I don't think people were into weights at that time like they are now. In fact, I know they weren't, but Cyrus was. I think he was as good with the ball in his arms as anybody we've had at Virginia Tech. He didn't have great hands, but as a true runner, he's the best I've had."

Above: Howard Lewis (25), Keith Lee (88) and John Luderman (69) weren't successful in stopping the Hokie offense in a 20-3 loss in 1981. (Photo Michael Bailey)

Right: UVa QB Todd Kirtley throws a pass in 1981. (Photo Michael Bailey)

There was speculation that Bestwick's time was up even before he was summoned by Virginia athletic director Dick Schultz on the eve of the 1981 Tech-UVa game. Schultz, who had played college baseball and coached college basketball, was not known for his football expertise. He had fired a football coach in his previous job at Cornell, and although that move went virtually unnoticed at the time, the man Schultz fired—George Seifert—went on to lead the San Francisco 49ers to multiple National Football League championships.

Schultz was not known as a hatchet man, however, and it was not his intention to fire Bestwick in their November 27, 1981 meeting. Bestwick had three years remaining on his coaching contract, and another two as an assistant athletic director. Schultz gave Bestwick the option of returning as coach for the 1982 season if he would agree to step down should the Cavaliers not win six games. Under this arrangement, he would be paid for only one of his remaining two seasons as coach. "Instinct told me it wouldn't work, but my heart told me I had to give him another chance," Schultz says. "There were some other things I wanted to talk over-such as staff changes and utilization—but we never got that far."

So, like Sonny Randle before him, Bestwick went into the final game of the season knowing it would be his last. The year had been difficult. The Cavaliers had lost five games by six points or fewer, including three three-point losses. The team had been ravaged by injuries, and Bestwick himself had been run over on the sidelines at North Carolina State, and now he faced certain knee surgery after the season ended. "To get this proposal to restructure my contract at 4:30 in the afternoon before the last game, it was kind of hard to get the team up," he says. "It was kind of hard to get myself up."

The football program was better for having had Bestwick. This is one reason Schultz was optimistic that he could convince a proven coach to take the job. The name of Navy coach George Welsh emerged almost from the start, although Welsh was a perennial prospect whose name also had been mentioned with openings at Pittsburgh, Arkansas, Tulane, Wisconsin, Florida, Georgia Tech, Notre Dame, and Duke.

Other names linked to the Virginia job included future ACC head coaches Bobby Ross, an assistant with the Kansas City Chiefs at the time, and Dick Sheridan, enjoying a successful tour at Furman. But Schultz never talked seriously with any candidate other than Welsh, a Navy alumnus who had compiled a 55-46-1 record at his alma mater, including four straight winning seasons and three bowl trips.

"**I**f this is a graveyard," said Welsh, referring to the unkind fate that had befallen his predecessors, "it's a pretty nice graveyard." But, Welsh later admitted he had underestimated the problems he would face upon his arrival at Virginia. Bestwick had gained a reputation as a "players' coach," a term usually taken as a compliment. In this case, the players had taken advantage of Bestwick's forgiving nature; they lacked discipline. In addition, Virginia had enjoyed so little success on the field that losing was almost a foregone conclusion, an attitude that did not escape prospective Wahoos.

If UVa had reached Tech's level by the late 1970s, the Hokies had clearly surpassed the Cavaliers by 1982. Nevertheless, for the second year in a row, Tech had suffered an embarrassing late-season loss—this time a 45-0 pasting at Vanderbilt—and had played itself out of bowl

Below: Tech fans tear down the goal posts following a 48-0 victory in 1983.
(Photo Dan Grogan)

contention by the time Virginia came to Lane Stadium on a bitterly cold Thanksgiving night. The teams had agreed to an 8:00 P.M. start to accommodate WTBS, the Ted Turner-owned superstation that would air the game. That decision was disastrous.

The weather wasn't the only problem. The Tech students, who generally turned out 15,000-strong for a good matchup, had gone home for the Thanksgiving break and not returned. That, combined with an anticipated blowout of a 2-8 Virginia team, kept the crowd to 23,800 for a game that two years earlier had attracted a record Lane Stadium crowd of 52,000. It was the first Tech-UVa crowd under 30,000 since 1970.

The game was about as impressive as the turnout. Tech's defense, ranked first in the nation against the run, lived up to its billing by holding the Cavaliers to 10 yards on the ground. The Hokies also intercepted five passes, one reason they were able to overcome a 7-6 halftime deficit and win 21-14. The only reason Virginia was even in the game was the spectacular play of senior defensive back Pat Chester, who returned an interception 33 yards to set up the Cavaliers' first touchdown, and who later had a 66-yard punt return nullified by a clipping penalty.

When WTBS showed interest in televising the Tech-UVa game in 1983, Virginia, the home team, balked at another Thanksgiving night kickoff. Schultz's decision to turn down a $500,000 offer did not have Dooley's support, but, as independents, the Hokies had more at stake. The Cavaliers would have been obliged to share their TV

Right: **Robert Brown records a sack in Tech's 30-0 win in 1980.** (Photo Gene Dalton)

Below: **Tech QB Steve Casey scrambles downfield.** (Photo Virginia Tech Sports Information)

Below right: **Gene Bunn picks off a pass in 1977.** (Photo Virginia Tech Sports Information)

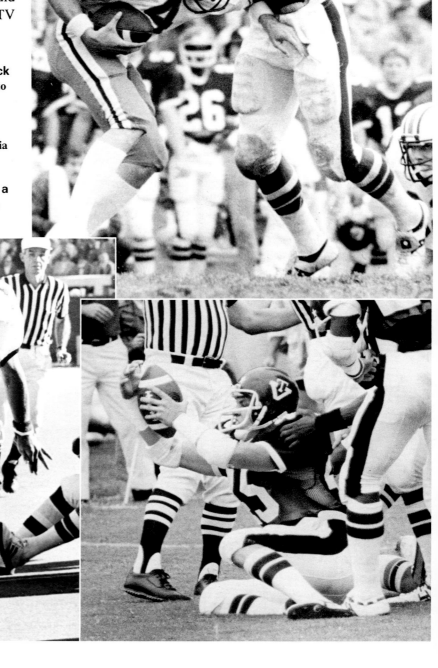

Above left: **Tony Paige sheds would-be tacklers.**
(Photo Bill Setliff)

Above: **Otis Copeland scurries through the middle of the UVa defense in Tech's 21-14 win in 1982.**
(Photo Virginia Tech Sports Information)

Below: **Mickey Fitzgerald, one of Tech's most celebrated recruits in the 1970s, rumbles through the UVa defense.** (Photo Virginia Tech Sports Information)

money with the rest of the ACC, but, more than that, there was the memory of 1982 and a half-empty Lane Stadium. That year, 1982, turned out to be an aberration; Tech-UVa games continued to attract record-breaking crowds.

After the departure of Cyrus Lawrence, Tech's marquee player was defensive tackle Bruce Smith, a 6-4, 275-pound behemoth so incredibly agile that he was the starting center for a state-championship basketball team at Booker T. Washington in Norfolk. Dooley never understood why Smith wasn't more heavily recruited. Coaches would flock to the Tidewater area, but they tended to ignore inner-city Norfolk, which did not have a reputation for producing big-time prospects—much less academically qualified big-time prospects.

"You got to make a call every year because you never know what's going to be there," Dooley says. "Michigan got in on him and so did [Ohio State's] Woody Hayes. The Big Ten got in there late on him. But, locally, I couldn't believe that no one was recruiting him. It was like Lawrence Taylor, when we were at North Carolina. I had to go up there [Williamsburg] and make a courtesy call. A guy said, 'You ought to come up here and take a look at him.' No one recruited Lawrence Taylor either."

By 1983, Smith had reached the prime of his

George Welsh is carried off the field after a 17-14 upset of No. 19 North Carolina in 1983. Only one week later Welsh would suffer one of the most embarrassing losses of his career— 48-0 to the Hokies.
(Photo Dan Grogan)

Right: UVa QB Wayne Schuchts (12) throws a pass. (Photo Grogan)

Below: Wayne Schuchts takes a snap during Virginia's 48-0 loss in 1983. (Photo Julie Heyward)

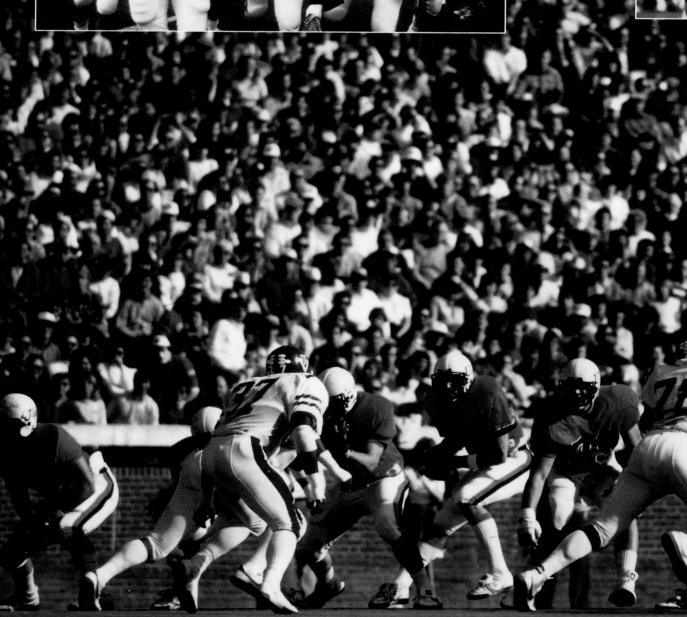

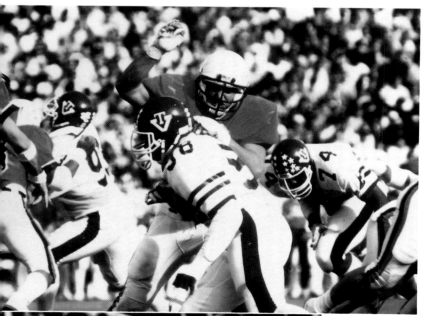

Mickey Spady eyes the
Tech defense.

Jeff Morrow (50) and Eddie Smith (73) celebrate
in the end zone at Lane Stadium.

Above: Mike Shaw rumbles six yards for a touchdown in 1982. (Photo Gene Dalton)

Below: Bruce Smith

Above: Bruce Smith was as feared as any man to play for the Hokies.

illustrious college career. He set a school record with 22 quarterback sacks and 31 tackles for loss. But he wasn't alone. Tech's leading tackler was Mike Johnson, an inside linebacker whose National Football League career would rival Smith's for longevity—12 years later, they remain major contributors—if not celebrity. Safety Ashley Lee, a product of the Hokies' recruiting pipeline to Southampton High School, was the other big name on a defense that shut out four opponents.

A season-ending game with Virginia received considerable buildup because it marked the first time in 42 years that both teams were assured of finishing over .500. The Cavaliers had clinched a winning season one week earlier with a 17-14 upset of 19th-ranked North Carolina, but that only served to enrage the Hokies. The Tar Heels, their hopes for a bigger bowl dashed, agreed to take a Peach Bowl bid—contingent on a victory over Duke—but only if Dooley and the Hokies weren't the opponents.

"How can North Carolina say they're not in our class?" Smith asked. "What it is is, North Carolina is afraid to play us. They know we would win." Then Smith turned his venom on the Cavaliers, who were suddenly being mentioned as a bowl team. "If any team doesn't deserve to go to a bowl, it's Virginia," Smith

Above: Cyrus Lawrence was
known for having big days
against UVa.

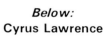

Below:
Cyrus Lawrence

said. "I can't understand how people are talking to
Virginia about going to a bowl when we might not be
going to one. We're a much better team than they
are."

Smith was right. The Hokies had 325 yards in total
offense in the first half, intercepted four Virginia
passes, and obliterated the Cavaliers 48-0 before the
largest crowd (44,572) in Scott Stadium history. Yet,
bowl officials found a way to overlook a team that won
its last five games, finished 9-2, and outscored the
opposition 301-91. The season-ending performance
was not unappreciated by the Tech fans, who streamed
onto the field and tore down the goalposts at the north
end of Scott Stadium. "They beat an injury-plagued
team," said UVa linebacker Charles McDaniel, lost
for the day after three-and-a-half minutes, "but they
didn't put in their second string until the end. Tech will
pay for this."

The Cavaliers and Hokies prepare to do battle.

Jason Wallace and an unidentified Hokie battle for
the ball in 1989 action.

THE CALL

CHAPTER 9

"For me, being from the Roanoke Valley, it was very big. The first time we played them, there was a Tech fan behind our bench who kept jeering at me, 'Toliver, you traitor.' "

—Elton Toliver, Virginia defensive end and linebacker (1985, 1987-1989)

For his first fifteen seasons as a collegiate head coach, George Welsh never had an offensive coordinator. He had been a quarterback at Navy, where he had led the nation in total offense in 1955 and finished third in balloting for the Heisman Trophy. His focus had been on offense as an assistant coach at Penn State from 1963-1973, and again as the head coach at Navy from 1973-1981, where he took responsibility for calling the plays. After practice each Thursday night, he would leave football behind. Early Friday morning, however, he would return to spend five or six hours fine tuning the game plan.

Welsh was in the middle of one of those sessions before Virginia's game with Virginia Tech in 1984, when he noticed on film that the Hokies invariably went to a goal-line defense when the opposing offense was in a short-yardage situation, even if it was nowhere near the end zone. "Most teams don't do that; we don't do that," Welsh says. "It's too risky. Something just popped into my mind and I made a mental note to look for that [alignment] the next day. If they were in that goal-line defense again, we would try and exploit it."

Herman Moore hauls down a pass against the Hokis in Scott Stadium.

The Cavaliers could use any edge they could get over a Tech team that had finished the 1983 season in such impressive fashion. Mike Johnson had graduated, but Bruce Smith was still on hand, and the Hokies still had an imposing defense. Tech had started slowly, with narrow victories over Wake Forest and Richmond sandwiched around a loss to West Virginia, but memories of a 48-0 romp over Virginia were fresh when the Cavaliers visited Lane Stadium on September 29 as 7½ point underdogs.

Above: The handwriting was on the wall for UVa. in a 30-0 loss to the Hokies in 1980.

Right: Tommy Vigorito gained 80 yards of total offense in the 1980 game.

Far right: Don Majkowski (1) hands off to Steve Morse (29). (Photo Dan Grogan)

The keeper of the flame in recent years has been Dave Braine, named athletic director at Tech on January 1, 1988. Braine came to Tech from Marshall University, having previously been an assistant football coach and an administrative assistant at Virginia. As he enters the 1995 football season, Braine has been a part of the Tech-UVa series for 14 years, seven at Virginia and seven at Tech.

"The most vivid memory I have is of the Jimmy Sharpe crew," says Braine, referring to the Hokies' head coach from 1974-1977. "The first time [1976] they were in Charlottesville, I remember coming out

Above: Kenny Stadlin made a 56-yard field goal against the Hokies in 1984. (Photo Dan Grogan)

...t: Ron Mattes (98) strips Tech QB Mark
...ox of the football. (Photo Dan Grogan)

...ow: Tom Kilgannon sacks Mark Cox.
Tech recovered the fumble.
(Photo Dan Grogan)

of the locker room and seeing their coaching staff sitting up in the back of a pickup truck. And, I thought, 'How unique!' Then, there was the game we tied [in 1977] and Tech was running the Wishbone. I was the secondary coach and I knew that the Wishbone with two split ends was the toughest thing to defense. Well, they came out in the second half with two split ends—they hadn't showed it all season—and we never stopped it.

"I also remember, as a recruiter, I lost a guy named Steve Wirt who came here [Tech] as an offensive

"I'm going to mention the score as a reminder," said Welsh at his weekly Monday news conference, "but, I'm not going to pass out any slips, like some coaches do. It'll be nothing like, 'Remember the Alamo,' or 'Payback,' a popular expression not too many years ago. Talk is cheap. If their personnel is better and they're playing well, they're going to win. I've been around for about 200 games now and that's the way it usually happens."

Clearly, the Cavaliers' personnel had improved. If Tech had the best defensive lineman in the country in Smith, UVa had one of the best offensive linemen in Jim Dombrowski, a 6-5, 300-pound tackle. "But," said Dooley at his midweek meeting with the media, "the big difference is their quarterback, [Kevin] Ferguson, has more ability than their quarterbacks in the past. By that, I mean he can run."

M uch of the pregame talk centered around quotes attributed to Virginia linebacker Charles McDaniel after the 1983 game. After implying that the Hokies had taken advantage of an injured Cavaliers' team and run up the score, McDaniel had a few irrational things to say about Bruce Smith. "If I told you what I think about Bruce Smith, you couldn't write it down," said McDaniel, who would have been well-advised to stop at that point. "I doubt Bruce Smith can even spell his name." It was no wonder that the Roanoke Times ran a photo of McDaniel in 1984 with a headline in big block letters: "WANTED?"

"I don't know if he's [McDaniel] a marked man," said center Mark Johnson, something of a Tech spokesman at the time. "I don't think we're going to set him up for a knee job or anything. If he thinks we're going to go after him . . . that's not possible, because if you try and double-team a linebacker, somebody else is going to make a big play somewhere else. More than anything, I think most of us wonder why he would say something like that.

"It's obvious McDaniel doesn't know Bruce. If he was trying to point at the stereotype of a big, dumb football player, he picked the wrong guy. Bruce is intelligent and articulate. . . . We really don't appreciate [McDaniel's] remarks and, if you think about it, it was pretty stupid to say that. You should never do anything to fire up the other team. There's no reason."

McDaniel realized his error as soon as he returned to his Fredericksburg home for Thanksgiving in 1983. He received fifty or more letters and several phone messages, one allegedly from Cavaliers' quarterback Wayne Schuchts. "My parents and I have separate lines," McDaniel said at the time, "and they gave the guy my number. The whole time I'm thinking, 'Why would Wayne Schuchts be calling me?' " Which, of course, he wasn't. "The guy never said who he was," McDaniel says, "but he must have called 10 times. There was a lot of derogatory stuff. After what I said, I guess I deserved some of it."

McDaniel was so embarrassed by the whole incident that he wrote a letter to his hometown paper, The Free Lance Star. "I explained the situation—that we were under a lot of pressure to win [in 1983] and that what I said was out of anger and frustration. I wrote that I was sorry for what I said. I love to play on Saturdays. When you don't have anything to say about the outcome, you're helpless. I didn't have anybody to hit, so I talked. Obviously, what I did was wrong."

W elsh was on edge—not an uncommon state—in the days leading up to the 1984 game. And, the drive to Blacksburg didn't do much to put him at ease. "On the way up here, I saw a new bumper sticker. 'Squeaker of the year . . . Tech 48, Virginia 0,' " Welsh says. "I don't know if the players saw it, but we kept passing the car and getting passed, so I saw it about three times."

lineman. And it completely devastated me. He was a very good student. He wanted engineering. It wasn't 'till later that I came to find out what a good engineering school Tech had. But, at the time, I couldn't believe I had lost a kid to Virginia Tech who was a good student.

"I'd been here several times for football and basketball games and really never thought it was that attractive a campus because all I had seen was the football stadium and Cassell Coliseum. When I came here and interviewed for the job, I was totally amazed that the place was so beautiful. I think that's still

Above: **Shawn Moore celebrates a TD against Tech.**

Left:
**Shawn
Moore
unleashes
a pass.**

And that was before they got to Blacksburg. "I remember the trip specifically because we had a police escort," recalls Welsh more than 10 years later. "We were on the interstate; then, once we turned off the interstate, the Virginia Tech police picked us up and it took an hour and a half, or some ungodly length of time, to get to the game. We were in the right-hand lane, with a police escort, and everybody was going past us. I thought it was deliberate. I mean, you had to suspect it. By the time we got to the stadium, I was furious. They didn't take us up to the gate. They dropped us off in the parking lot and we had to endure the insults of the Virginia Tech fans as we walked to the locker room."

It may have served as motivation for Virginia. The Wahoos overcame an early 6-3 deficit to take the lead on an 18-yard pass from Don Majkowski, who had taken over for an ineffective Ferguson, to freshman wide receiver John Ford. The Cavaliers stretched their lead to 13-6 on a school-record 56-yard field goal by Kenny Stadlin before the half. "You mean, he kicked a 56-yarder?" Welsh asked the media after the game. "I thought it was 52 [yards]. If I'd known that, I probably wouldn't have kicked it. We'd have thrown a Hail Mary pass or something."

In a questionable strategic move, Welsh sent Ferguson back out for the second half, promptly losing

true today with so many people in the state of Virginia; Virginia Tech is perceived . . . as a country-bumpkin type of university, basically because of our location.

"Speaking only from the perspective I had as an assistant football coach and assistant [athletic director] at Virginia, basically I felt we had a better university. I felt like we had a more quality operation and that we were doing things the right way, doing things with class. That was looking at things through Virginia eyes. A lot of people in Charlottesville think of this as a cow college. People here feel that a lot.

any momentum the Cavaliers had gained with Stadlin's field goal. Tech intercepted three Ferguson passes, the last resulting in a touchdown on a 17-yard return by Bob Thomas. Then, Eddie Hunter ran for a 17-yard touchdown early in the fourth quarter. With just 10:48 remaining, down by 10, the Cavaliers faced fourth-and-inches at the Tech 34.

Majkowski, after faking a dive, went for the bomb but thought he had overthrown Ford. So did Welsh. Ford, listed at 6-3, left his feet around the 5-yard line and was almost horizontal as he gathered the ball in his fingertips. An impressive burst of speed allowed Ford to catch up to the ball, but intense concentration enabled him to maintain control as he hit the ground. "The way he stretched out and caught that ball, he looked like the Rubber Man," Dooley says. "I shall never forget it. It was *unbelievable*, just an unbelievable catch."

Though Ford did not score on the play, Beaver Petty hit the end zone one play later on a 1-yard run. Following a missed two-point conversion attempt, the score remained 23-19. The Cavaliers took the lead when Ford caught a 14-yard touchdown pass from Majkowski with 5:07 remaining. They sweated out a 52-yard field goal attempt by Don Wade as time expired. "I overcompensated," says Wade, who already had kicked three field goals. "All I had to do was kick it 50 yards with the wind and I tried to kill it."

The fourth-and-inches call has been hailed as the turning point in the Cavaliers' football program ("Without that play, Virginia may still be Virginia," future Tech and UVa assistant Phil Elmassian said), but Welsh isn't so sure. He remembers a 3-8 record that left UVa at another crossroads following the 1986 season. Still, there is no denying that the victory over Tech in 1984 catapulted the Cavaliers toward one of the most memorable seasons in school football history,

The UVa bench eruputs after Kenny Stadlin's 56-yard field goal to end the first half in 1984.

Don Majkowski takes a snap from center against the Hokies.

This spectacular diving catch by John Ford on fourth-and-inches spurred the Cavaliers to their come-from-behind win in 1984.

of the Wahoos look down their noses at us and that is why it's such an intense rivalry for us. In the last four years, I think you've seen more genuine respect and an end to some of the stereotypes."

Braine doesn't think there is any question that his UVa ties helped him get the job at Tech. At the same time, Braine hopes that none of his coaches underestimate how fervently he wants to beat Virginia. It was perhaps the crowning accomplishment of the Braine Era when Tech was able to align itself with the Big East for football, but he wants nothing to detract from the games with Virginia. At the suggestion that

Tech QB Mark Cox tries to elude the pressure of Tom Kilgannon.

difference. We kicked the hell out of Duke [38-10] the next week. Then, after that, we got on a roll. But, I remember telling the staff before the Tech game, 'We've got to beat these guys one of these years. How else are we ever going to be able to recruit in the state and hope to get the best players?'

Tech didn't exactly fall apart after the Virginia game. The Hokies took out their frustrations the next week in a 54-7 romp over VMI, one of five straight victories before they fell to Clemson 17-10 in the 10th week. At the conclusion of an 8-3 regular season, Bruce Smith was honored with the Outland Trophy as the nation's top lineman and the Hokies were rewarded with a bid to the Independence Bowl. But there was one problem: Smith was ineligible for postseason play, the result of 12 relatively minor infractions committed by the Hokies in 1983. Smith won a court order to play in the bowl game—in which Air Force beat the Hokies 23-7—but Tech's shenanigans wouldn't be forgotten by the NCAA.

T he Hokies entered the 1985 season without Bruce Smith, Ashley Lee, and Jesse Penn—ringleaders of dominating defenses the previous two years—and the early results were not promising. Tech opened with three straight losses, including games they were expected to win at Cincinnati and against Richmond in Blacksburg; they dragged into Charlottesville with a 2-4 record. The Hokies were 11-point underdogs, the first time since 1979 that they had not been favored over UVa.

Virginia, at 3-2, had failed to live up to some expectations, but the Cavaliers still had an explosive offense that featured Majkowski, Ford, alternating tailbacks Barry Word and Petty, as well as Dombrowski, who would become UVa's first consensus All-American in more than 40 years. There were some questions how the 'Hoos would respond to a 27-24 setback at

one in which they lost their opening game to Clemson 55-0 at home and didn't lose again till the regular-season finale.

"I don't know about the players, but it finally showed me that we could beat Tech," says Welsh, no doubt unaware that the Cavaliers hadn't won in Blacksburg since 1970. "Our confidence level went sky-high after that, I thought, which made a big

the schools do not give the rivalry the credit it deserves, Braine is quick to interrupt. "I think we do," he says. "They don't look at it the way we do. Our rivalry with Virginia is bigger for us than their rivalry with us is for Virginia."

For Braine, it cheapens the rivalry if the teams play any time other than the last game of the season. Both Virginia and the ACC would like to see the Cavaliers play a conference team on the last weekend of the regular season. But, Tech and Virginia have signed contracts that specify that the game will be

George Welsh took the UVa program to national prominence.

Clemson, their 26th straight loss to the Tigers, but these were seemingly answered when Virginia outgained the Hokies 241-49 in taking a 10-0 halftime lead.

The deficit was not so insurmountable that Tech abandoned its gameplan, however. After forcing Virginia to punt on the first series of the second half, the Hokies scored on their next four possessions, virtually reversing the first-half statistics, outgaining the Cavaliers 249-41 en route to a 28-10 triumph. The Hokies ran the ball on 23 straight plays for a combined 200 yards from the "Stallions," alternating tailbacks Eddie Hunter and Maurice Williams, in what Roanoke columnist Bill Brill termed "the sweetest win" of Dooley's eight-year Tech tenure.

"I used to have a terrible time with heat," Tech defensive back

played in late November until the year 2000—an arrangement that Braine will not alter unless the Cavaliers agree to move their men's basketball series to campus sites. "To me it's very irritating," says Braine of UVa's eagerness to play the football game earlier in the season. "If I were in the same shoes, I'd do the same thing, but you saw what happened last year."

In 1994, the Cavaliers originally were scheduled to play North Carolina State in October, but moved the game to November 25, the Friday after Thanksgiving, when ABC offered an 11:00 A.M. national

Above: Ray Savage looks to maul a Tech ball carrier.

Right: Shawn Moore rolls out in a 16-10 victory in 1988.

Below: John Ford hauls in a pass as a freshman.

Above: Shawn Moore and Durwin Greggs (40) on the offensive.

Below: Cavalier coaches and players celebrate during a 26-23 victory over the Hokies in 1984.

television appearance. The Cavaliers, showing none of the crispness that marked their 42-23 victory over the Hokies six days earlier, blew a 12-point lead and lost to the Wolfpack 30-27 in a decision that cost them a bid to the Fiesta Bowl or another high-paying postseason game.

Virginia coach George Welsh has been quick to counter any suggestion that the Cavaliers do not view the Hokies in the same light as some of their conference opponents.

"I was reluctant to say we've got to put everything into this game because we've got one to follow."

Flanker Marcus Mickel carries the ball in 1989 action. (Photo Mark Nystrom)

Carter Wiley says. "I used to go to the hospital all the time after games for dehydration and I can still picture the scene at halftime—me sitting in the corner, soaking in ice, and listening to Dooley. He was damn near challenging every one of us personally. [He was] walking up to every one of us and saying, 'Is this the way you play football? Is the way you want to be remembered? Is this who you are?' He raised our ire enough to go out and make a run of it again in the second half. There was not anything devious or ill-directed. Dooley always just tried to get each one of us to come together to make something happen."

Welsh, disturbed by his team's second-half performance, put his players off limits to the media the following week for the first time in his 3½-year tenure. "A game like this is difficult to swallow," he said, "but it's probably going to happen again if I stay around much longer ." (He was right.)

The Cavaliers never developed any consistency and finished a disappointing 6-5. Even Word, who was the ACC player of the year, and rushed for a school-record 1,224 yards, could not pull them out of their slump. Tech had the same record but fewer complaints; after a predictable 35-18 loss at Florida, the Hokies won their last three.

By the time Tech entertained Virginia in 1986, the Hokies knew they were playing their final season under Dooley. Rumors of possible recruiting violations once more attracted the attention of the NCAA, and Tech administration support for Dooley eroded. Tech proceeded with plans to replace Dooley as athletic director, causing an acrimonious dispute. Ultimately, Dooley challenged the decision in a $3.5-million lawsuit.

In the days leading up to Virginia's October 25 visit, there were stories in the newspapers about formation of a 23-member search committee and about a proposed settlement of Dooley's lawsuit, but the Hokies had shown an admirable ability to stay focused, going 4-0-1 after a season-opening 24-20 loss to Cincinnati. Strong but not invincible, Tech lost a 29-13 contest to Temple the week prior to their UVa showdown.

UVa's Welsh was quick to dismiss the Temple game. "I don't think it makes any difference what Tech did last week." he said. "They've always played well against us, whether they've just won or just lost, whether they've had a good team or they're struggling."

Besides, Welsh had his own problems. The Cavaliers had taken a step backward after posting three staight winning seasons. They entered Lane Stadium with a 2-5 record. To make matters worse, Majkowski had a bruised right (throwing) shoulder that had kept him out of action since September 27.

Majkowski had a capable backup in Scott Secules, later an All-ACC quarterback, but Secules took a helmet to the thigh at the end of the first quarter. The Hokies, up 14-0 were ready to pounce on their wounded prey. "I wasn't sure I wanted to play Don Majkowski before the game," Welsh says, "but, once Secules' thigh started to tighten, I had to get him out of there." Majkowski did not aggravate his injury significantly, but questions about his arm persisted. He slipped to the 10th round of the NFL draft later that spring.

Tech, after three years of going back and forth between quarterbacks Mark Cox and Todd Greenwood, had turned over the offense to junior Erik Chapman. Chapman tossed a first-quarter touchdown pass to Donald Wayne Snell, but, as usual, there was more than enough work for senior tailbacks Eddie Hunter and Maurice Williams. Williams had 18

said Welsh before the teams played in 1994, "but I've changed my thinking. We've got to let it all hang out. . . . We've got to do everything we can to win this game and then deal with next week on Sunday."

In retrospect, Welsh isn't sure that the Cavaliers were able to maintain the fire that burned so intensely against the Hokies. "That's why I've wanted to play the game in the fourth or fifth week of the season [and] still do," he says. "I don't see what we gain by playing it at the end. It should be the same thing for them in their conference. Why not play West Virginia?"

Above left: QB Kevin Ferguson prepares to throw the football in the face of the Hokie pass rush. (Photo Dan Grogan)

Above middle: The UVa victory in 1984 was the first in Blacksburg since 1970. (Photo Dan Grogan)

Above right: Kevin Ferguson fires the ball down the field. (Photo Dan Grogan)

Below left: UVa LB Charles McDaniel's (30) remarks after the 1983 game only added to the intensity of the 1984 contest. (Photo Dan Grogan)

Below: UVa bench celebrates a 26-23 win in 1984. (Photo Dan Grogan)

"There's just something about that game last year. It would have been better for us to lose to Virginia Tech and beat North Carolina State than vice versa. Playing [the Hokies] in that kind of game and then coming back to play State on Friday . . . we weren't the same team."

Some say the rivalry never meant as much to Virginia because the Cavaliers traditionally had more out-of-state players. That might have been true during the 1960s and early 1970s, when ACC teams were limited in the players they could recruit by an 800 minimum on the Scholastic Aptitude test—but as

Above left: John Ford heads for the end zone in 1987 action. (Photo Dan Grogan)

Above right: Chris Stearns tries to run down a Hokie ball carrier. (Photo Dan Grogan)

Right: The Cavaliers huddle during a 14-13 victory in 1987. (Photo Dan Grogan)

Below right: UVa assistant coach Ken Mack (blue sweater) enjoyed the 1984 celebration. (Photo Frank Selden)

scholarship limits were imposed and there was greater parity in academic standards, UVa reached its greatest heights with in-state players like Shawn Moore, Herman Moore, Terry Kirby, and Chris Slade.
After Welsh was hired as Virginia coach in 1981, the first prominent in-state player to sign with the Cavaliers was Charles McDaniel, a linebacker from James Monroe High School in Fredericksburg. Though he had made an oral commitment to North Carolina and would not have signed with Virginia had Welsh not been hired, once he signed, there was never a more passionate Wahoo.

Tight end Steve Johnson makes a spectacular touchdown reception in 1989. (Photo Dave Knachel)

Webb said. "That's the type of people they recruit. They quit." It was similar to the outburst by Virginia linebacker Charles McDaniel two years earlier, except that McDaniel's comments came after a Cavaliers' loss. Like McDaniel, however, Webb was injured early in the game and might have been talking out of frustration. In any case, by the time the Hokies had their weekly Tuesday news conference, a letter was on the way to Welsh from Webb.

"It was a poor show of sportsmanship and lack of couth," wrote Webb, who claimed his remarks had been taken "out of context. . . . I simply meant that once we got ahead by 17, I didn't feel the momentum could change that

Maurice Williams is tripped up by the UVa defense. (Photo Matt Gentry)

carries for 143 yards and Hunter rushed 25 times for 130 yards; in their careers, they rushed for a combined 784 yards against Virginia (Williams 404, Hunter 380).

"It was probably our worst game of the season," Welsh said after the 42-10 loss, "but every time I say that, it's like I'm not giving Tech enough credit." Welsh did not question his team's effort ("You get so far behind, what the hell do you expect?" he observed), but even the Cavaliers allowed as how they might have given up. Not surprisingly, the Hokies couldn't resist an opportunity to get in a few jabs.

"Everybody knows, when you get Virginia down by 17, it's pretty much over," Tech nose guard Mark

Hokie fans have had an aversion to McDaniel since 1983, when, in a fit of frustration after a 48-0 loss, he questioned whether Tech star Bruce Smith could spell his name. McDaniel says he received almost 100 calls—so many, in fact, that his parents had to change their phone number—and the Roanoke Times heralded the 1984 game by printing a picture of McDaniel that was framed to resemble a "wanted" poster. More than a decade later, McDaniel regrets some of his earlier phraseology, but he hasn't changed his feelings toward the Hokies.

much with that kind of time left." Webb was properly contrite when trotted out to the news conference, but teammates hinted that the apology was forced. "I always told the players to act with class," said Dooley later. "If you ever say anything about an opponent, it's nothing but praise. Don't ever say anything derogatory. Of course, looking at it from the other side, you've [the media] got to have something interesting for the readers."

Before he responded to Webb's comments, Welsh had to deal with a statement attributed to Cavaliers' defensive end Sean Scott. "I don't know what the problem was," Scott said after the game. "Oh, yes, I do. We gave up in the second half." Welsh dismissed Scott's remarks as a cop-out, but conceded that UVa needed a new approach against the Hokies, who'd won six of the last seven games against the Cavs.

Erik Chapman puts the moves on a Cavalier defender in 1987.
(Photo Dave Knachel)

"When I came here, somebody told me Virginia Tech had all those Virginia kids, some couldn't get in here and they were angry," he said. "I don't buy that. But, if people do have [that perception], it's helping them and not helping us."

C learly Tech was on a mission that had nothing to do with Virginia. It began the Friday before the Hokies' third game. Dooley called the players together in Syracuse to inform them that he had been forced out as Tech coach. It was school president Bill Lavery's contention that he intended only for Dooley to step down as coach, but that didn't matter to the players. The Hokies responded with a 26-17 upset victory over an Orange team that featured quarterback Don McPherson, and future NFL players Darryl Johnston and Tommy Kane.

"Total inspiration," is the way tight end Steve Johnson described it. "I don't know how many people knew it, but, from that point on, several players sported headbands with Lavery's name on them. At that point, Jim McMahon was hip and he was doing all that stuff. It was like, 'Here, take this!' We were angry. There was a lot of anger directed at the management of the university. We were determined, from that point on, to have the very best season we

"You follow one or the other," says McDaniel, who still holds the UVa record for tackles in a career with 432. "If you're a Virginian, you don't follow both. I don't know many people who have ever switched. I started with Virginia, I was with Virginia growing up and, obviously, I went to school there. Since then, I've had a brother and sister go there. I grew up wanting to play in the Tech-Virginia game. I had seen so many of them and, no matter how bad Virginia was, there was always something special in the air for that ballgame. I just wanted to be a part of that."

could for Bill Dooley."

The record books credit Tech with a 10-1-1 record—the only ten-win season in school history. It should be noted that the loss to Temple was reversed when star running back Paul Palmer was found to have signed with an agent, but the Hokies won their last five games, including a 25-24 triumph over North Carolina State on Chris Kinzer's dramatic game-ending field goal at the Peach Bowl.

"We remained extremely focused and it revolved around Bill Dooley's talk with us [at Syracuse] and his consistent and timely remarks to us in team meetings, cautioning us to ignore all the peripherals that don't mean a damn," says Johnson. "One of his strengths was his ability to keep a team focused on the task at hand. I hated to see him go. I really did. I loved that man. As many knocks as he took, he was a good football coach and a good individual."

It was an awkward situation till the end for the players, who, when they weren't practicing for the Peach Bowl, were reading daily of the search for a new coach. New athletic director Dutch Baughman, previously the associate commissioner of the Southwest Conference, immediately went after Bobby Ross, who had resigned as Maryland's coach December 1. When Ross could not be persuaded to take the final step, the search centered on two former Hokies: Temple head coach Bruce Arians and Frank Beamer from Murray State.

UVa cheerleaders at Scott Stadium.
(Photo Dan Grogan)

Once he had removed his name from consideration, Ross tossed his support behind Beamer, who had coached under him at The Citadel. Arians, who probably knew he wouldn't get the job, grew weary of the process, and pulled out of the race December 21— three days after his interview. Baughman had spoken with former Wake Forest head coach Al Groh, but it was no big surprise when Beamer was introduced December 23, 1986, as Tech's 32nd head football coach.

Beamer, 40, had compiled a 42-23-1 record in six seasons at Murray State. If the Hokies were impressed, they didn't show it; many of the players remained attached to Dooley. "I like Frank Beamer and I think he's doing a great job," Steve Johnson said in the summer of 1995. "He's a fine man and I don't have a problem with Frank. The problem I had was, we had a winner going and, for whatever reason, it was disrupted. Any time you have change, you have disgruntlement. The seniors-to-be did not view that [disruption] favorably. Like everything else, when there's change, it takes time to get into the ebb and flow of the system."

Virginia already had lost two games when it entertained the Hokies (0-1) on September 19, 1987. What was worse, the Cavaliers had a quarterback controversy. Fifth-year senior Scott Secules had started the first two games, but talented freshman Shawn Moore had thrown a second-quarter touchdown pass in a 21-

McDaniel was among a group of Virginia players who were the first to play on consecutive winning teams (1983-1985) in more than thirty years. The Cavaliers were only 1-3 against Tech during his career, however, so he has had to live vicariously through subsequent UVa teams and annually stages a big party for friend and foe during the week before the Tech game. In 1994, when a friend was getting married on the same weekend that the Hokies and Cavaliers were playing, McDaniel flew into Blacksburg for the game and then flew back to the midwest for the conclusion of the wedding ceremonies.

Above: Cavalier fans sing "Good Old Song."
(Photo Dan Grogan)

Right: The Cavaliers bid the Hokies adieu in 1987.
(Photo Dan Grogan)

19 loss to Maryland, causing some to wonder why Welsh went back to Secules in the second half. "I don't mind the second-guessing," Welsh said. "I don't care what you write. I'm just tired of answering the same old questions: 'Why are you using two quarterbacks? Why do you take them out when one guy's hot and why do you put 'em in when the other guy's hot?' Those kind of things."

Secules tightened his grasp on the starting job when he completed his first seven passes, including touchdown passes to Keith Mattioli and Tim Finkelston, putting UVa went up 14-0. Tech, which had rushed for 356 yards against UVa less than 11 months earlier, picked up only 124 this time. Nevertheless, the Hokies wouldn't die. With 1:24 left in the game, Johnson made a spectacular diving TD catch to bring them within one.

"What I mostly remember was that the pass [from Erik Chapman] wasn't for me," Johnson said of the 14-13 Virginia win. "It was actually called for Karl Borden. I was trailing the play by about 30 yards. A buddy of mine put together a video and it shows the whole thing. Instead of making the interception, the defensive back batted it and I dove from just inside the goal line and caught it with my fingertips. There's a

"It's probably not a healthy thing to do, and my wife doesn't understand it, but if I'm driving along and I see a Tech bumper sticker or a Tech license plate on a car, I've got to pull ahead of that car," says McDaniel. "I always try to pass or get in front of that car, so they see on my back windshield, 'Virginia . . . The University,' which really pisses most Tech people off. My wife thinks I'm insane. My daughter now says, 'Daddy, there's a Virginia Tech car.' Even if I'm driving by myself, I do it to amuse myself."

(Continued on page 168)

Eddie Hunter attempts to shed Cavalier defenders. (Photo Matt Gentry)

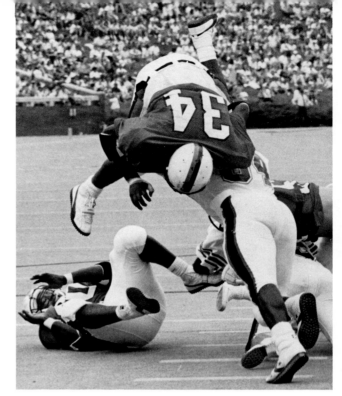
Tech's Victor Jones upends the UVa ball carrier.
(Photo Virginia Tech Sports Information)

photo that shows my hands clearly underneath the ball, although Welsh will go to his grave saying the ball hit the ground first."

The catch was every bit as sensational as John Ford's catch for Virginia in 1984, "but we didn't win," Johnson says. "If you win the game, it's a huge factor. If you lose the game, it's just another play." Dooley went for the win, but tailback Malcolm Blacken didn't get out of his backfield before he was swarmed by Elton Toliver, Jeff Lageman, and a host of other Cavaliers on an attempted two-point play. It marked the third time in 14 years that the Tech-UVa game had been decided by a two-point play at the end of the game, not counting the 1977 game that ended in a tie. Every other time, the Cavaliers emerged victorious.

The Virginia defenders were on top of Blacken so quickly, they seemed to know the play. In fact, they did. Toliver, then a sophomore defensive end, later admitted that one of the Tech linemen was tipping the Hokies' plays before the snap. "That wouldn't surprise me," Johnson says. "You would think, as quick as they jumped on us, something bad went wrong. I remember watching the play on film and just shaking my head. The sad thing is, the key to a sweep working

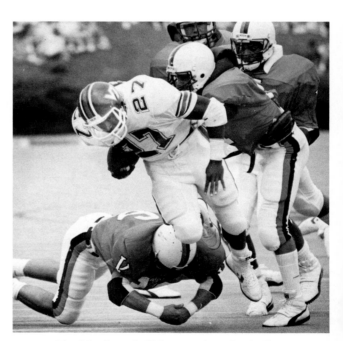
Tech's Jon Jeffries carries the ball.
(Photo Dave Knachel)

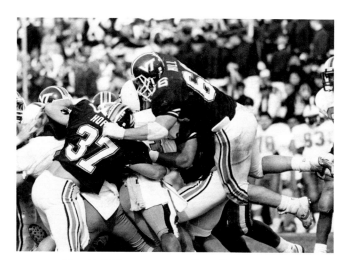

Scott Hill swarms a Cavalier runner.
(Photo Dave Knachel)

Chris Kinzer kicks the ball in a 14-13 loss in 1987.
(Photo Virginia Tech Sports Information)

Lawrence White makes the initial hit while Victor Jones (34) and Rick Singleton (99) come to help out.
(Photo Virginia Tech Sports Information)

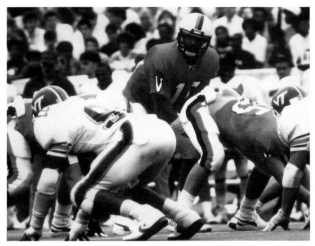

Scott Secules under center in 1987 action.
(Photo Jon Golden)

Cavalier fans celebrate in 1989. (Photo Dan Grogan)

Ray Savage (56) prepares to attack.
(Photo Jon Golden)

Shawn Moore hands off to Terry Kirby in 32-25 victory in 1989. (Photo Frank Selden)

is the tight end's block. I had my guy pinned. That sucker was in the back of the end zone."

"The guard had been leaning," Toliver says. "Not terribly, but you noticed the tendency every now and then. On that particular two-point conversion, he was just rolling out of his stance, so I shifted to his inside shoulder and shot the gap. I went on my own. It was all instinct. I'd been doing a lot of guesswork; I remember coach Welsh saying something about it. It paid off sometimes and sometimes I got burned. There was definitely a team effort on that play because I wasn't the only one back there."

It was the first of three straight victories for the Cavaliers, whose 1987 season is viewed as a turning point by Welsh, though not for anything that happened in the first part of the year. From the time they lost 58-10 to South Carolina, where cancer-stricken former player Craig Fielder died on the eve of the game, the Cavaliers won their last four regular-season games and then defeated Brigham Young 22-16 in the All American Bowl. The Hokies went the other direction, losing six games in a row before beating Cincinnati 21-20 to finish 2-9.

It was not the best of times for Tech's athletic program, which learned October 27 that it had been placed on two years' probation by the NCAA. The Hokies were found to have exceeded Division I-A football scholarships by 36 over a three-year period under Dooley, who termed the infraction "an honest mistake" that did not give the Hokies a competitive advantage. Nevertheless, Tech was prohibited from awarding more than 17 new football scholarships for the 1988-1989 school year (the limit was 30) or having more than 85 scholarship players in the program (the limit was 95) over a two-year period.

Dooley by then had received a $1-million annuity as settlement of his lawsuit and was in his first year as the head football coach at Wake Forest. Lavery, blamed for a variety of athletic department ills, resigned October 16—eleven days before the release of the NCAA report. Gone, too, was athletic director Dutch Baughman after only five months. Beamer, forced to deal with a bad situation not of his making, knew things could get worse before they got better. The Hokies struggled to a 3-8 season in 1988.

That didn't prevent Tech from throwing a late-season scare into Virginia, something of a budding power when it visited Lane Stadium on October 29, 1988. In a sign of things to come, UVa freshman wide receiver Herman Moore caught seven passes for 175 yards, including a 9-yard touchdown pass from Shawn Moore that put the Cavaliers ahead 13-10 at the half. Herman Moore, a 7-foot high jumper, scored the touchdown on what would become his signature move-an "Alley Oop" play on which he outjumped a smaller defender. A field goal by UVa's Mark Inderlied represented the only scoring of the second half, but that didn't bother Welsh. "Only at Virginia are you loved when you're 4-4," he said.

Marcus Wilson takes the ball upfield.

Left: The 'Hoos and Hokies mixed it up before the 1989 contest.
Below: One-time Hokies' recruit Herman Moore (No. 87) receives considerable attention from Tech defenders.

Below: A look of uneasiness comes over the UVa sideline in 1989 as Tech trims a 24-0 deficit to 32-25.

Left: Herman Moore had two of his three biggest games against the Hokies.

Right: Wide receiver John Ford set up one touchdown and scored twice on receptions in UVa's 26-23 victory in 1984.

Left: The UVa "Pep" Band survives despite an irreverent brand of humor that opponents don't always find charming.
Below left: Randy Cockrell and others can't stop UVa's Terry Kirby from scoring.
Below right: Terry Kirby holds ball aloft after scoring touchdown in UVa's 32-25 win in 1989.

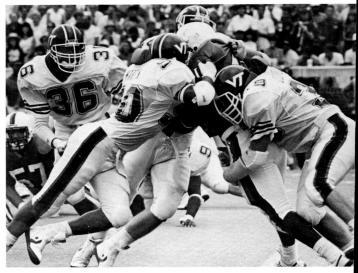

Above left: Myron Richardson takes it on the chin. (Photo Bob Hines)

Above right: Bobby Martin (90) and Randy Cockrell (39) combine to make a tackle. (Photo Bob Hines)

Left: Tech's Lamar Smith walks over a UVa defender in 1987. (Photo Dave Knachel)

Right: The Hokie Bird shows his contempt for the Cavaliers. (Photo Gene Dalton)

Below: Jim Dombrowski.

Battle of the Bands

The Tech-UVa football game almost always coincides with Commonwealth Day, an occasion for officials from both schools to meet and socialize with the governor. In 1988, then-Governor Gerald Baliles was on hand in Blacksburg and came down to the field at halftime to recognize Vernell "Bimbo" Coles, a Tech basketball star who had played on the United States Olympic Team that summer.

Both bands were scheduled to play, including UVa's self-proclaimed Award-Winning Virginia Fighting Cavalier Indoor/Precision Marching Pep Band and Chowder Society Revue. The "pep" band, known more for its mischievous skits than its music, made some predictable off-color jokes about Coles' nickname and then announced that he would be given the keys to the water treatment plant.

"They had some guy run out on the field wearing a torn T-shirt with 'Bimbo' written on it," then-Tech basketball coach Frankie Allen said. "I was so upset, I just walked out. I could have understood if maybe they'd driven a tractor out there, but when it's a personal attack on an individual, it goes beyond good humor. Nobody knows how hard this kid had worked. When it was his day to be recognized by friends and family, they made a mockery of it."

Jim Copeland, Virginia's athletic director at the time, hadn't left the stadium before he was accosted by irate Tech supporters and the complaints escalated until UVa officials conducted an official review of the performance. Associate director of athletics Kim Record, admitting that the review board was unaware of the governor's special presentation, said the band would send an apology to Coles. "We've got to eliminate . . . the pep band during the season," UVa coach George Welsh said.

In 1993, the athletic department put an end to the halftime skits, and the pep band boycotted a newly formed University Sports Band for the first five games. University officials and band members declared a truce on the eve of the Virginia Tech game. UVa officials informed the Marching Virginians, as Tech's band is called, that they would not be able to take the field before the game or at halftime; the previous year, the UVa Pep Band had been banned from taking the field at Tech.

Amid charges of "payback" from the Marching Virginians, Tech athletic director Dave Braine begged off. "Hey, I'm not going to touch it," he said. "I tried to make a deal with Jim Copeland and the deal couldn't be worked out. I understand Jim's problem. Jim and I don't have a problem."

Terry Kirby had a lot to smile about after going 3-1 against the Hokies during his tenure at UVa. (Photo Dan Grogan)

THE

KNOCKOUT

"I never root for them. I don't care who they're playing. They could be playing Iraq and I would root for Iraq."

—Cam Young, Virginia Tech quarterback (1988-1989)

Virginia Tech quarterback Cam Young was in no mood for chatter after the longest and most painful day of his college football career. Finally a starter in his fifth season, Young had reached for a first down in the third quarter against Virginia and his right arm had snapped in two places. Taken by ambulance to UVa Hospital, he received a pain-killing nerve block, and then drove three hours to Blacksburg for surgery at Montgomery County Regional Hospital. "There I was, with my right arm in two pieces," he recalls, "and one of the nurses came up and asked, 'Hey, Cam, did they ever find Frank's tooth?' I had no idea what she was talking about."

It was four or five days before Young learned what had happened. As UVa was attempting to run out the clock in the closing moments of a 32-25 victory, simmering

Shawn Moore poses with the Heisman Trophy at the Downtown Athletic Club in 1990.
(Photo David Greene)

hostilities reached a boil between linemen on both sides of the ball. Hokies' defensive end Jimmy Whitten isn't sure who delivered the first shot—he concedes that it might have been he—but within moments of the final horn, there was a full-scale melee involving players, fans, and other assorted pugilists. Tech head coach Frank Beamer was anxious to be a peacemaker, but found himself ill-protected.

"I'm thinking that I don't want to see it end like that," Beamer says. "I can tell it's dangerous. All the people are coming over the walls and there's so much that could go wrong. So, I run out. And, I'm going to grab Jimmy. But, Jimmy doesn't see me coming. If he had seen me coming, I don't know if it would have made any difference. He's got the guy and, just as I get there, he draws back and his elbow gets my [right front] tooth. It wasn't a real strong

tooth to begin with. I'd gotten it knocked loose in a high school basketball game.

"So, there went the tooth. I guess 'stunned' is the best word for my reaction. My wife [Cheryl] is up in the stands. She sees me running and, all of a sudden, I go down. Now, remember, this is the year [1989] that I had my heart problem at East Carolina. Finally, she spots me and I'm on my knees, but she thinks it's my heart again. She goes, 'Oh, my gosh!' I think that was the last time she's been to Charlottesville. And, she's not going back again. Just too many bad memories."

"W hen you first feel up there after a tooth's been knocked out, there's a hole and it feels like there've been three teeth knocked out," Beamer says. "And I'm like, 'Geez, we came up here and got our tails kicked and now this!' But one thing it does is, it stops the fight. Jimmy turns around and

asks, 'Coach, are you all right?' I say, 'Yeah. I've got something missing here, though.' This is a heckuva thing. I'm walking around there and I see [director of media relations] Jack Williams and I say, 'I don't know if I can do an interview.'

"All this time, the tooth is on the rug, with all the students running around and celebrating. Our team dentist [Dr. Howard Stanton] says, 'I believe, if we can find the tooth, we can get this thing taken care of.' So there they were, 45 or 50 minutes after the game, out there looking for my tooth. Finally, somebody brought it back and they were able to glue it in, so at least you could talk. I sounded so different. Then you look at yourself in the mirror and all of a sudden there's a gap in there. Ugh."

Beamer subsequently was fitted for a bridge, but the broken tooth disappeared somewhere along the way. ("We're trying to forget that day," says Beamer, whose office is filled with other memorabilia). That was fine with Whitten, whose career was marked by several confrontations with Virginia, many of them in print. Though it wasn't readily apparent that Whitten had knocked out Beamer's tooth—speculation at first was that a UVa player or fan had done the damage—

(Continued from page 157)

Virginia Tech fans might be pleased to know that the first thing McDaniel does on Sunday mornings during the fall is to check the sports page to see how the Hokies have fared. "If Tech wins, then Virginia better have won, or else it's a bad day," he says. If McDaniel has a counterpart in recent Tech-UVa history, it is former Hokies' defensive end Jimmy Whitten.

Whitten didn't grow up as a Hokies' fan at George Washington High School in Danville, nor did he harbor any ill feelings toward Virginia. But he was an emotional player, and once he chose Tech, he got

Whitten knew he was the culprit.

"I felt somebody jump on my back," says Whitten, now a graduate student in counseling and an assistant strength coach at Tech. "I assumed it was a player or a fan. I turned around, looked down, and there was Coach Beamer on the ground. He was a little bit out of it and I couldn't tell he didn't have his tooth. Then, I saw Dr. [Duane] Lagan on the ground looking for Coach Beamer's tooth. We were all on our hands and knees, amid all these students and all this fighting, looking for a tooth.

"The last thing I remembered was, I looked up and here was this coach from UVa. I think it was [Tom] O'Brien, a red-haired guy. And he said, 'Look what you've done to your coach,' like I'd done it intentionally. I was glad we beat those suckers the next year, although I kinda kept my mouth shut. I guess it's good to be remembered for something, but I thought I had a pretty good career and played for some pretty good teams. I hate to be remembered as the guy who knocked out Frank Beamer's tooth."

The 1989 game almost went down as the greatest comeback in the history of the series. Virginia had entered the game as a nine-point favorite and a crowd of 44,300 was preparing for a premature departure as the Cavaliers increased their lead to 32-8 with 4:04 remaining in the third quarter. UVa's home field advantage was greater than usual since Tech's ticket allotment had been cut to 5,114. "You could have offered me a couple dozen Top Flight XLs

right in the middle of the rivalry. The Cavaliers hadn't recruited him, "but I couldn't care less," Whitten said in an interview before the 1987 game. "I didn't want them to recruit me." Then, he went on to say the Cavaliers were dirty and trash talkers and that their fans were ill-behaved.

"My perception of UVa didn't start immediately," says Whitten. "I dressed out for the '86 game [when he was being redshirted] and I didn't see what the rivalry was all about. We beat the stuff out of them [42-10]. Then, the next year we got beat and there was a lot of mouthing. Regardless of where I was, I

(Continued on page 172)

(Continued on page 172)

Above: P.J. Killian forces a Maurice DeShazo fumble. (Photo Dan Grogan)

Below left: DeShazo eludes the pressure of Tom Burns. (Photo Dan Grogan)

Below right: Chris Slade recorded five sacks against the Hokies in 1991. (Photo Dan Grogan)

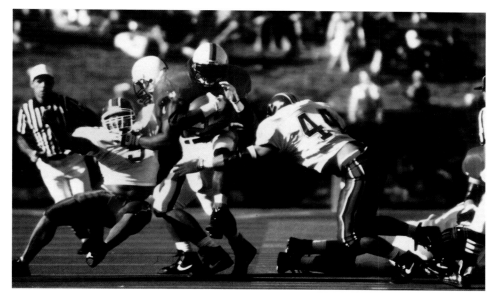

Top: Terry Kirby waltzes through the middle of the Tech defense.
(Photo Frank Selden)

Middle: Matt Blundin threw for 222 yards and three TDs against Tech in 1991.
(Photo Frank Selden)

Bottom: Nikki Fisher tries to avoid the Hokie defense.
(Photo Frank Selden)

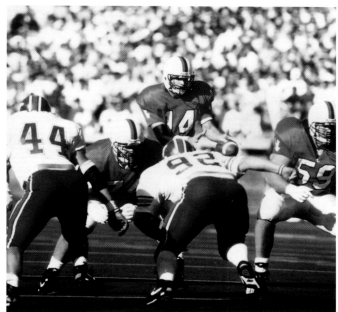

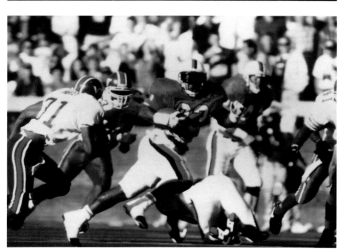

and I still couldn't have gotten you a ticket," says Tech ticket manager Tom McNeer, a golfer of modest ability.

The contract between the schools specified that the visiting team would receive no fewer than 4,500 tickets (since lowered to 3,800), but Tech's allotment had once been over 10,000. The change came with Virginia's success; the Cavaliers began to sell more than 20,000 season tickets. Demand was so great for the 1989 game that Virginia associate athletic director Jim West says the Cavaliers could have sold 65,000 tickets if they had the available seats. UVa (8-2) had won eight of nine games and had moved into the Associated Press rankings at number 18, while Tech, on the verge of its first winning season under Beamer, was 5-3-1.

The Hokies did not begin their comeback until Rodd Wooten, previously the third-string quarterback behind Young and injured regular Will Furrer, entered the game in the third quarter. The Hokies were on the move when Young reached for the ground to steady himself on an option play and UVa defensive tackle Joe Hall was blocked into him by Tech offensive guard Skip Pavlik. "What I'll always remember is that Bo Campbell had dropped a ball in the end zone two plays earlier," Young says. "I've always kidded Bo, telling him if he catches that ball, I don't break my arm."

It was one of the most gruesome plays in a Tech-UVa game or any other series, reminiscent of the broken leg that ended the career of Washington Redskins quarterback Joe Theismann. "It was the most painful thing I've ever been through," Young says. "Eugene Chung walked over and said, 'Cam, get up.' He tried to pick me up, then saw my arm, and dropped me right on the spot. I saw [Virginia linebacker] Ray Savage later that winter and he said he almost got sick." Another UVa player, Elton Toliver, says he was looking at the arm when it snapped. "It's something I'll never forget," Toliver says. "Everybody was yelling, 'Somebody get over here.' It was terrifying."

The 1990 football season was like no other in Virginia football history. The Cavaliers won their first seven games, were ranked number one in the country for three weeks, and inspired talk of a national championship with a high-powered offense that featured Heisman Trophy candidate Shawn Moore at quarterback, All-American Herman Moore at wide receiver, and a 1,000-yard rusher in Terry Kirby. In the background, like a nagging toothache, was the realization that Virginia Tech was lying in wait in Blacksburg, where the teams were to meet in the final regular-season game.

The Hokies were only 5-5, but they were coming off a 6-3 loss to eventual co-national champion Georgia Tech. They were not intimidated—not by Virginia, not by anybody. The Cavaliers (8-2) were struggling at this point, having blown two-touchdown leads in losses to Georgia Tech and Maryland. They entered Lane Stadium without Shawn Moore, who had suffered a dislocated right thumb the previous week against Maryland. Understudy Matt Blundin had NFL size (6-7, 235 pounds) and an NFL future, but UVa was a shaky six-point favorite.

As the Tech coaches pulled into the parking lot in back of the Jamerson Athletic Center, they were greeted by a curious sight. There the players were,

sitting on the curb, applying black paint to their shoes. The Hokies didn't have black shoes at the time, so the seniors had gone out the day before the game and purchased the paint. Tech equipment manager Lester Karlin was livid, but it was clear that the players could sense a big win and wanted to make a fashion statement in the process.

In his office, Beamer was experiencing little of the uneasiness that usually leads up to gametime. "It was a four o'clock game, the Friday after Thanksgiving," Beamer says. "I remember coach [Jerry] Claiborne walked into the office the morning of the game and we were talking. He said, 'You know, you're really calm to be getting ready to play Virginia this afternoon.' And, I was like, 'You know, I just feel good about the game.' Our practices had gone well. We were playing pretty well. Those feelings are hard to explain sometimes. And, they don't always work out. I've felt pretty good about some other games. . . ."

The Hokies, decked out in all-maroon uniforms for the first time since 1984, scored on four of their first five possessions and led 24-6 at the half. Vaughn Hebron, out of most of the previous four games with a groin injury, had a career-high 31 carries for 142 yards. And, freshman cornerback Tyronne Drakeford intercepted two passes deep in Hokies' territory. But, nobody could have enjoyed the game any more than junior quarterback Will Furrer, who passed for 254 yards and three touchdowns. Virginia had recruited Furrer when he was at Fork Union Military Academy, but the Cavaliers said they could take only one quarterback and backed off an undecided Furrer when Brian Satola decided to commit. "Furrer never forgot it," UVa coach George Welsh says.

Blundin passed for 305 yards—the only 300-yard game of his college career—but was intercepted three times. Virginia had a season-high six turnovers and the Tech students in a state-record crowd of 54,157

(Continued from page 169)

liked the competition and the rivalry part of it. It's no fun if you're not going to be kind of hateful. But, to this day, I still don't like 'em at all. It was nothing against any player. It's the schools. It's like two different worlds."

Tech affiliates were left with a strange dilemma in 1990: Virginia won its first seven games and was ranked No. 1 in the country for three weeks. Most true Tech fans have difficulty pulling for Virginia under any circumstances, but UVa had to come to Blacksburg in the last week of the season and, as the Cavaliers

reveled in the Cavaliers' misery, tearing down the Lane Stadium goalposts after the game. "Once again, it's such a game of momentum," Beamer says. "We had it rolling pretty good and they had just lost a tough one to Maryland the week before. They lost Shawn Moore in that game, too. So, it was like it was just set up for us to win that game. It seems like whoever's playing with a new quarterback is going to have a tough time."

Losing to the Hokies didn't prevent Virginia from receiving a bid to the Sugar Bowl, where the Cavaliers led Tennessee until the final thirty seconds before losing 17-16. That was in the days before the Football Bowl Coalition, when bowl committees would start getting itchy in early November. Welsh is convinced that UVa deserved its midseason billing, at least offensively. But, the Cavaliers were never the same after All-ACC tight end Bruce McGonnigal injured his spleen in a mysterious, off-field accident after the sixth game.

The letdown that resulted from four losses in the last five games had just worn off when the football program suffered an even greater indignity. At mid-

Bo Campbell reels in a 49-yard reception against UVa in 1990. (Photo Dave Knachel)

afternoon on Friday, May 17, 1991, UVa faxed out a one-page news release in which it acknowledged the possibility of rules violations. Jim Copeland, who had become athletic director in 1987 when Dick Schultz resigned to become executive director of the NCAA, said there was evidence that the Virginia Student Aid Foundation (VSAF) had made approximately three dozen loans to student athletes between 1982 and 1990.

Virginia had not been totally scandal-free. On the eve of the 1986 season, the United States Attorney's Office in Charlottesville confirmed that three Virginia football players—1985 ACC player of the year Barry Word, All-Conference placekicker Kenny Stadlin, and running back Howard "Beaver" Petty—had been charged with conspiracy to distribute cocaine. All three served jail time and Petty, the only one of the players with remaining eligibility, was suspended for his final season. As much embarrassment as that caused the school, the department, and the program, it was an in-house matter that did not require the intervention of the NCAA.

The loan case was another story. After an 11-month

were ringing up fifty points nearly every week, most people looked at Tech as having the best opportunity to knock them off.

"People were always saying, 'We'll be the only ones who beat 'em,'" Whitten says, "but, man, I just hate 'em so bad that I was glad when Maryland beat 'em. I remember we had an off week and I was sitting there in my apartment, watching the game by myself. I was just rooting my butt off for Maryland. Maybe that was just my mentality. I think a lot of the guys wanted to see [the Cavaliers] come in here undefeated.

Moore Heartbreak for Hokies

Herman Moore caught 17 passes for 505 yards in three games against Virginia Tech and each one felt like a dagger to the chest. Hokies' fans knew his story by heart. Moore, pen in hand, had been preparing to sign with Tech when he abruptly changed his mind and picked bitter rival Virginia.

Moore became an All-American for the Cavaliers and a first-round draft pick of the Detroit Lions, but his early career was somewhat less illustrious. He was the place-kicker for George Washington High in Danville as a junior, not starting at wide receiver until his senior year. He was better known for his exploits in track and field and was not rated one of the top 25 football prospects in Virginia,

Other prospects made their decisions early, so, as the national signing day approached, Moore was one of the state's top uncommitted players. Maryland expressed an interest in him early, but Moore scheduled his last two visits to Virginia and Virginia Tech—not a bad position for the schools, provided the prospect didn't cancel his visits.

Moore liked his visit to Virginia and seemed destined to become a Wahoo, but he was equally impressed by his trip to Blacksburg, where his host was former George Washington teammate Jimmy Whitten. Moore had decided he was going to sign with the Hokies before learning of an article in the Richmond Times-Dispatch, reporting that Tech would not accept "partial" qualifiers.

Moore was a good student, but he had not made a score of 700 or better on the Scholastic Aptitude Test, as required for freshman eligibility. At the time, Virginia did not have a policy

Above: In three games against the Hokies, Herman Moore caught 17 passes for 505 yards.

Below: Detroit Lions first-round pick Herman Moore leaps into the air.

for partial qualifiers—eventually, the Cavaliers and the rest of the ACC would share Tech's position—but they had looked at Moore's transcript and figured there was a good chance he would make the score, although they were prepared to accept him without it.

That was good enough for Moore, who went over 700 on the first testing date after the signing period and never had any problem academically at Virginia. Indeed, he graduated in four years—before his eligibility had expired. Nevertheless, as late as Moore's final year, people were taking shots at Virginia for accepting him.

"I wish I could show you Herman's transcript," says Tom Fletcher, an administrator at Tech who had recruited against Virginia for fifteen years at North Carolina and Tech. "He was a good student and he had taken good courses. Once he got the test scores, he had the credentials to be admitted to almost any school that plays Division I-A football. It would be an absolute crime to suggest anything else."

Two of the three biggest receiving days of Moore's career were against the Hokies, although the last came in a 38-13 loss to the Hokies in 1991. "I didn't blame the kid," says Tech Coach Frank Beamer, who had been at Tech for less than two months when Moore was proposed for admission. "I remember telling our admissions people, 'We're going to live to regret this.' I think it was something that affected both programs. Herman Moore was really a tough guy from an area where Virginia Tech had been pretty strong. I think he had an impact on other people coming through and he certainly had an impact on our series the next four years."

Above: **Randy Neal intercepted two passes and returned both for touchdowns against the Hokies in 1992.**
(Photo Frank Selden)

Right: **Jerrod Washington rushed for 133 yards and a TD in a 20-17 loss to the Hokies in 1993.**
(Photo Walker Nelms)

explaining possible NCAA violations. "This is a sad day in our institution's history. It is fair to say the reputation of our university has been severely tarnished."

In an accompanying report to the NCAA, Virginia confirmed that it had disassociated itself with two VSAF officials who had approved loans, former executive directors Ted Davenport and Joe Mark, and said that associate athletic director Jim West had accepted early retirement. The UVa study indicated that West had directed the student athletes to VSAF, although he showed no memory of that in interviews with investigators. There would be other victims, most notably Schultz, who resigned as NCAA chief within days of the May 7, 1993 announcement that UVa had been placed on probation.

internal investigation, Virginia made public the contents of a 529-page report that revealed a total of 78 loans, totalling $47,000, made to student-athletes, graduate assistants, and other students. "They were not available on the same terms to all students and they did not have a repayment schedule," said president John Casteen,

Many, including rival Virginia Tech, thought the Cavaliers got off easy. Virginia was restricted to 86 scholarships for the 1993 season and 83 for 1994—two under the NCAA limit in each case. In addition, the Cavaliers lost one of its two allotted graduate assistant coaches for one year, but there was no ban on postseason play or television appearances. Virginia was cited for violations in 13 different areas, but received less than the proscribed minimum penalty because of its cooperation with the NCAA and a history of good behavior.

The NCAA sanctions were an embarrassment, but caused little disruption in the

but I'd just as soon see them get up a lot and lose. I just don't like them. I have as much fun rooting against UVa as I do rooting for Tech now. Even when Tech wasn't doing well, I could look at a UVa loss and think, 'That's great.'"

It isn't easy to find people with connections to both schools. Eric Hairston, a promising defensive lineman from the Martinsville area, enrolled at Tech in 1984 and later transferred to Virginia, although he never played in the Tech-UVa game. Twins Tiki and Ronde Barber, whose father, J.B., was a Tech

Tight end John Burke celebrates Tech's 1993 win over the Cavaliers. **(Photo Dave Knachel)**

straight weeks beginning with the second game. This was followed by a four-game home stand. Tech won the first three of those home games and improved its record to 5-4, raising hopes for a bowl bid as East Carolina visited Lane Stadium in Week Ten.

Furrer had injured his right knee the previous week in a 42-24 victory over Akron, but was expected to play against East Carolina. Fifteen minutes before the game, he was doing little more than shifting his weight when the knee locked—on the side opposite the previous injury. There was speculation all week that arthroscopic surgery would enable Furrer to play against Virginia, but he spent the next Saturday afternoon in street clothes, never having played in Scott Stadium. "I've always wondered about that green patch in the middle of the field," he observed in typical offbeat fashion.

The Cavaliers rolled to a 38-0 victory—their biggest margin over Tech since 1952—as defensive end Chris Slade enjoyed one of his greatest games in a UVa uniform, with five sacks and a total of six tackles for loss. A sprained ankle had left Slade on crutches at midweek, but he was inspired by comments, attributed to Furrer, that Slade hadn't laid a hand on him in the 1990 game. "I thought about it all week," says Slade, who caused one fumble and recovered another. "Matter of fact, I thought about it all year. I told coach [George] Welsh that I was going to be out there even if it meant putting a turf shoe on one of my crutches."

Redemption was no less sweet for Blundin, who passed for 222 yards and three touchdowns and completed the season with a Division I record 224 pass attempts without yielding an interception. "It was a

Virginia program and certainly nothing to rival the drop-off experienced by Virginia Tech after it was put on probation in 1987. The Cavaliers came out of the first three games of the 1991 season with a 1-2 record, including a 17-10 victory over unimposing Navy, but had every excuse for a rebuilding year. Gone were the Moores, Bruce McGonnigal, most of the defensive line, and three starting defensive backs.

Tech entered the season with high hopes, based in no small part on the return of Furrer, who was on pace to break school passing records held by Don Strock since the early 1970s. The Hokies' schedule was not conducive to a fast start. They were on the road for five

running back in the early 1970s, have become major contributors for UVa. There are no known cases of brother playing against brother, although players for both teams have had siblings go to the other school. Mike Brancati, a Cavaliers' defensive back in the 1970s, has three brothers who graduated from Tech. "One is neutral, one became a big Virginia fan, and the youngest can't stand UVa," Brancati says.

But no one has felt both sides of the rivalry as acutely as Phil Elmassian. In fact, there are few in-state rivalries Elmassian hasn't experienced. Elmassian, a native of Wellesley, Massachusetts, played at

(Continued on page 179)

(Continued on page 179)

The Recruiting Wars

Tom Fletcher, who recruited in Virginia for more than twenty years, held the theory that most college prospects are going to consider one state school or another. That decision is going to be made prior to their senior year, at which point their final choice is going to come down to some out-of-state school and either Tech or UVa, but probably not both.

History provides considerable evidence to support that view; however, with Tech's 1991 football entry into the Big East Conference and continued success for both programs, the Hokies and Cavaliers are waging more and more recruiting battles, few more memorable than the 1993 contest for defensive end Cornell Brown from E.C. Glass High School in Lynchburg. Brown's final choices came down to Tech, UVa, and Maryland.

Brown's older brother, Reuben, had gone to the University of Pittsburgh, where he would become an All-American offensive lineman and eventual first-round draft pick. When Reuben was arrested for selling cocaine one week before his brother's 1993 signing day, Oglessa, the boys' mother, had reservations about Maryland. She was uncertain she wanted to send another son to a metropolitan area.

If the signing day had come one week earlier, Cornell would have signed with the Terrapins. Now, he was having second thoughts. Virginia Tech had caught his eye when four Hokies' players showed up to watch him play in a basketball game for Glass at Patrick Henry High School in Roanoke. His visit to Virginia was unremarkable, though as late as the morning of his press conference, he was said to be leaning to the Cavaliers following a call from his older brother.

His mother once had worked at the UVa hospital and reportedly favored the Cavaliers, but not even she knew what was coming when her son stepped to a microphone and announced, "I'm going to the University of Virginia," then, after a pause, "Tech." A gasp was heard from family and friends, still not sure what they had heard. "He shocked me when he said Tech at the end," Brown's mother says. "He says, 'University of Virginia,' and I said, 'Thanks, that's where I wanted him to go.' Then he said, 'Tech,' and I said, 'Wait a minute.' "

Brown was rated one of the top five prospects in the state by the Roanoke Times & World-News— the first top-five recruit to sign with the Hokies since 1990. The Hokies were to get two more top-five players in 1994, when they signed Group AAA player of the year Ken Oxendine, a running back from Thomas Dale High School in Chester, and quarterback/defensive back Tony Morrison from Indian River High in Chesapeake. It was a big blow for the Cavaliers, particularly since Oxendine was a frequent visitor to Scott Stadium as a youngster. Two days later, the Cavaliers got their own prize—Group AA player of the year Anthony Poindexter, a defensive back from Jefferson Forest High outside Lynchburg. Poindexter chose the Cavaliers over both Tech and North Carolina.

"I thought Poindexter had a great visit," Tech coach Frank Beamer says. "Knowing the family and just knowing the whole situation, I just thought we were going to get him. I'll tell you this, I'm not wrong on many. He came down here for a visit, we were in his home the next Monday or Tuesday night, and I told our coaches on the way back, 'We're going to get this guy.' Then, he went up to Virginia the next weekend and committed on his visit.

"With Cornell, I think I was like everyone else. One day, I thought he was going to Maryland. The next day I thought he was going to Virginia. Then the next day, I said, 'Well, maybe he is coming to Virginia Tech.' I don't know if he knew exactly where he was going to go. But last year, only two kids in the state visited here and Virginia. We got one (Sussex Central defensive back Tyron Edmond) and Virginia got one (Spotswood linebacker Dillon Taylor). If we can just keep the best players in the state, we can both be in the top 25."

Above left: Stacy Henley breaks up a pass. (Photo Dan Grogan)

Left: Baron Spinner unsuccessfully attempted to intercept this Cavalier pass. (Photo Dan Grogan)

Above right: Maurice DeShazo tossed five interceptions in his last home game, a 42-23 loss to the Cavaliers in 1994. (Photo Dan Grogan)

Above: Virginia Governor George Allen, a UVa graduate, tries to show impartiality before the 1994 contest. (Photo Dan Grogan)

Right: Tiki Barber carries the ball in 1994 action. (Photo Dan Grogan)

low point for me because it was the only game I had a hand in," says Blundin of the 1990 game. "Today's game was just the opposite—everything from how we played to the weather. It did mean a lot for me personally to prove I could play against that defense."

One of the unusual aspects of the Tech-Virginia series, at least in recent years, has been the success enjoyed by the visiting team. Since 1984, the visiting team has won six of 11 games, including the last three, ignoring crowds that have grown larger and more partisan with the success of the programs. This is consistent with the way Virginia, in particular, has played under Welsh. From 1991-1993, there was a period in which the Cavaliers lost only once in the span of nine road games. "We've been preaching that for a long time," Welsh says. "If you don't win on the road, you're not going to be a good football team."

In 1992, Virginia was reeling as it came into Lane Stadium. The Cavaliers, who had won their first five games under unheralded fifth-year quarterback Bobby Goodman, blew a 28-0 lead against Clemson in Charlottesville, losing 29-28, and were to lose four of their next five. A near-certain bowl bid had fallen out of reach and there was little at stake for the Cavaliers or Hokies, who were in an 0-7-1 tailspin that had included one-point losses to Rutgers (50-49) and the previous week to Southern Mississippi (13-12).

Virginia's slide had coincided with the absence of starting running back Terry Kirby, enjoying his best season until he suffered a broken shoulder blade against Clemson. Injuries were a major story line in 1990, when Virginia lost Shawn Moore, and 1991, when Furrer was out for the Hokies. While there was little doubt that Kirby would play, his effectiveness was questionable. He had carried 17 times for 61 yards the previous Saturday in a 31-7 loss to North Carolina State, when he appeared to be favoring his shoulder

(Continued from page 176)

Ferrum College and William and Mary, and then coached at Richmond. He later served on the Tech staff for two years under Bill Dooley (1985-1986) before moving to Virginia for four years. He returned to Tech in 1993 as defensive coordinator and coached in a total of eight Tech-UVa games—four on each side—before taking a position this past winter at the University of Washington.

"I think the biggest change, whether it's George Welsh or Bill Dooley or Frank Beamer, is that it's great to see the teams finally play when both were ranked in the top 25," says Elmassian, referring to

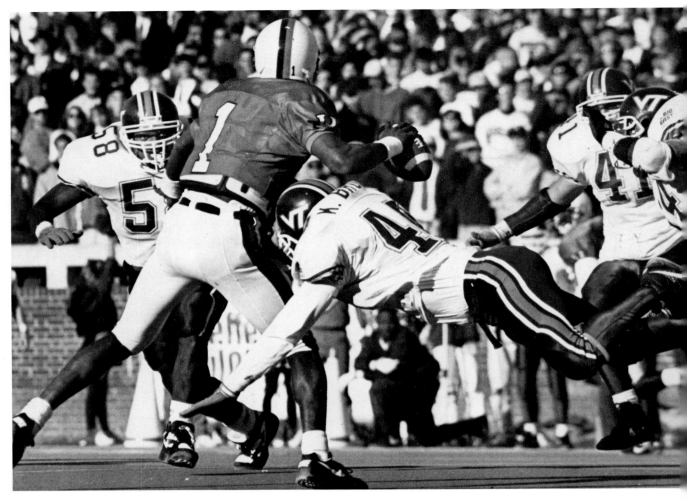

Ken Brown (44) and Cornell Brown close in on UVa QB Symmion Willis. (Photo Dave Knachel)

and was replaced in the fourth quarter.

It was out of respect, as much as anything, that UVa running backs coach Ken Mack said he would do what he could to get Kirby the seventy-six yards he needed to break John Papit's school rushing record. But Kirby didn't need sympathy. Earlier in the season, he had rushed for more than 200 yards in back-to-back victories over Duke and Wake Forest, but those were lopsided UVa victories. Against the Hokies, he carried

twenty-six times for 185 yards—many of these in the fourth quarter, when the Cavaliers needed every inch in holding off the Hokies 41-38.

Tech actually outgained the Cavaliers 573-344 and had possession of the ball for more than 35 minutes, but UVa got 21 points from its defense and special teams. Redshirt freshman Kareem Martin, added to the traveling squad after an injury to another player, blocked a punt that led to a Kirby touchdown run. The

the 1994 game, when Tech was ranked number fourteen and the Cavaliers were sixteenth. "Even when I was at Richmond, we beat Tech twice. When I played at William and Mary, we beat [Tech and] Don Strock. I'm really proud of the fact that I'm the only one who's gone to bowls with both teams and won em."

Elmassian once had another distinction. Until the Cavaliers beat the Hokies last year in Charlottesville, no team had lost a Tech-UVa game with Elmassian on its coaching staff. Coincidence had a lot to do with

score was 31-17 in the third quarter.

On the next possession, sophomore linebacker Randy Neal stepped in front of a Maurice DeShazo pass at the Tech 30-yard line and returned it for a touchdown—Neal's second interception-turned-touchdown that day, both from the same spot on the field.

Neal was to become known for his interceptions—he finished his career with ten interceptions, counting bowl games and two-point plays—but the interceptions against Tech were the first of his college career. At least one publication named Neal as its national defensive player of the week, which was something of an embarrassment, he later conceded, because the Cavaliers had given up so many yards and points. "I got handled by this guy [Tech center Jim Pyne] the whole game," Neal says. "No matter what I did, he was there. I wasn't happy after the game because I knew I hadn't really done what I was supposed to do."

After the 1992 season, the Beamer regime was at a crossroads. The 2-9 and 3-8 records in his first two years were tolerable, even understandable, in light of the NCAA sanctions and turmoil that carried over from the end of Bill Dooley's tenure. Athletic director Dave Braine and Tech fans weren't as understanding following a 2-8-1 season in 1992 and staff changes resulted. Casualties included defensive coordinator Mike Clark and longtime assistants Tommy Groom and Keith Jones. One-time Beamer teammates Duke Strager and Larry Creekmore had left after the 1991 season.

The defense was handed over to former Dooley assistant Phil Elmassian, who had left Tech under less than favorable circumstances in the purge of 1986. From there, Elmassian went to Virginia as a linebackers coach, but had to leave in 1991 to help make room for new defensive coordinator Rick Lantz. Elmassian surfaced at Syracuse, but it was during a spring fact-finding mission to the University of Washington that he was to form the attacking philosophy that he imparted to the Tech defense.

"I think it suits my personality; it's something I had been missing," Elmassian says. Obviously, it suited the players' personalities, too, because they won six of their first eight games and carried a 7-3 record to Virginia for the final regular-season game. Much of Tech's success came from junior Maurice DeShazo, who had been described by Beamer as "the best option quarterback in the country." DeShazo also was passing well; he set a school record with 22 touchdown passes, including four each against Temple and Maryland.

It was the Tech defense, however, that made—and saved—the day against Virginia. Although the Cavaliers were winning the statistical battle, Tech jumped to a 17-3 lead when freshman defensive end Cornell Brown hit UVa quarterback Symmion Willis and caused a fumble. Defensive tackle Jeff Holland promptly recovered and returned the ball 8 yards for a touchdown. ("Good thing it was eight," Beamer says. "I'm not sure he could have gone 18."). Virginia cut the deficit to 17-10 by the half and was on the move again before stalling at the Tech 7-yard line in the third quarter.

The Cavaliers were preparing to kick a field goal when an official's flag went flying. "Everybody was yelling at the kicker," Tech linebacker George DelRicco says, "but they called it on me. They said I was taunting. I'm thinking, 'Oh shit!' That gives them a first down." That's what everybody thought, but it was not an automatic first down. The Hokies were penal-

that, but Elmassian's coaching style was to work himself and his players into a frenzy and nothing got him more riled up than the sight of an archrival. "No matter who we were playing, 'Elmo' had his motor going at full speed," Beamer says, "but when we got ready to play Virginia, he shifted into another gear."

Elmassian isn't sure he agrees totally with that assessment, but he concedes that the 1987 Tech-UVa game—his first with the Cavaliers—was one of his most difficult experiences in coaching. "We had just won the Peach Bowl [at Tech] with those same kids on the field that day and it was killing me," says

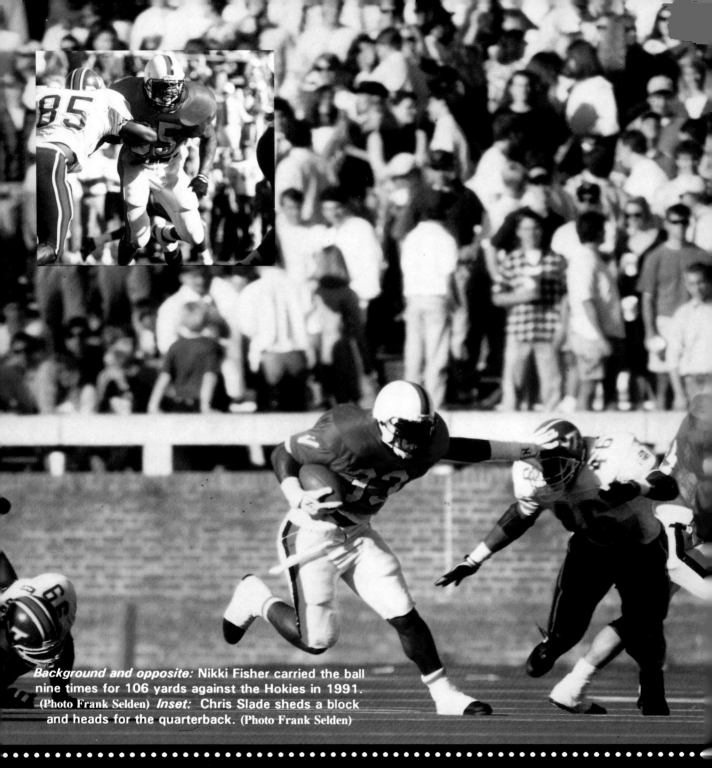

Background and opposite: Nikki Fisher carried the ball nine times for 106 yards against the Hokies in 1991. (Photo Frank Selden) **Inset:** Chris Slade sheds a block and heads for the quarterback. (Photo Frank Selden)

Elmassian, whose wife, Diane, is the daughter of former Tech equipment manager and thirty-five-year employee "Hokie" Reid Arrington. "I was happy for us and the [Virginia] players [after a 14-13 victory], but, boy, was it a sad day, especially after what we had gone through the year before."

"Virginia Tech has always had the mentality of a blue-collar, roll-your-sleeves up, bring-your-lunchpail program," Elmassian says. "That's me. And that's how it is. Hey, we're all Virginia rejects. Half the Virginia Tech football team, if they'd gotten a scholarship to Virginia, probably would have gone

Inset: Chris Slade revels in a 38-0 UVa triumph. (Photo Frank Selden)

there, [mid-1960s linebacker] George Foussekis included. They say, 'Well, I'll go Virginia Tech,' and they find out it's a great place. Then it's, 'Ok, let's go kick their fanny,' and for years, they did."

Elmassian says he frequently thinks back on the 1985 game, when Virginia had future National Football League players in Don Majkowski at quarterback, Barry Word at running back, and Jim Dombrowski at offensive tackle, as well as a future all-pro running back, Chris Warren. The Hokies prevailed 28-10 in Charlottesville. "The next year, we're out on the field before the game and one of their coaches says, 'Boy,

Tech's All-America center Jim Pyne.
(Photo Virginia Tech Sports Information)

ized half the distance to the goal, leaving Virginia with fourth-and-one at the three. Now the Cavaliers had to go for the first down, but Jerrod Washington was stopped in his tracks by freshman "rover" Torrian Gray.

As frequently happens, the details have been obscured by time. Many have forgotten that there was actually more than a quarter to play, and that DelRicco knocked down a Willis pass to end UVa's final threat. The Cavaliers were left to wonder how things might have been different if All-American offensive guard Mark Dixon had been available and they had run left instead of right on that fateful fourth-down play. Dixon had been suspended the day before the game for academic negligence, "but, as a coach, you never believe something like that until you see it," Beamer says. "In warmups, you're always looking around to see if there's somebody with his number (65) out there."

For only the second time, Virginia Tech and Virginia each received bowl bids following the 1993 season. At first, it looked as if the Cavaliers would stay home following a 7-4 season, but a spot opened in the Carquest Bowl in Miami, which had the fifth choice of teams from the Southeastern Conference, a conference that did not have five teams with the required six wins over Division I-A opposition. That had the predictable, irritating effect on the Hokies, who were to receive $700,000 from the Independence Bowl, while Virginia was headed for a $1 million payday from the Carquest Bowl. It was more than a little consolation when Tech blasted Indiana 45-20, one day before Boston College trounced Virginia 31-13.

Bowl bids were on the line again in 1994, when the Cavaliers visited Lane Stadium on November 19. It was originally scheduled as the last game for both

you've got some good-looking kids.' And I'm like, 'Hmmm, want to trade?'"
Steve Hale, who was at Tech from 1984-1991 as a walk-on center and graduate assistant coach, likes to tell a story about the 1986 game. "We were down in the halftime house [below the Lane Stadium stands] before the game and Elmo was ranting and raving," Hale says. "He said, 'You should be so fired up that you would take a baseball bat and go beat on the door to UVa's locker room and dare them to come out.' I think if there had been a baseball bat sitting there, Carter Wiley would have gone over and done it. Then

teams, but Virginia had agreed to shift an earlier game with North Carolina State to the Friday of Thanksgiving weekend for an 11:00 a.m. slot on ABC. Scouts from the Fiesta, Gator, Peach, Carquest, and Independence bowls watched the Cavaliers capitalize on eight Tech turnovers for a 42-23 victory, an unexpected outcome in a game that was close—19-13—at the half.

Nobody was more excited than UVa placekicker Rafael Garcia, a one-time Spanish exchange student whose father was seeing him play college ball for the first time. Garcia had such a bad practice week that he feared the Cavaliers would punt in any situations requiring more than a chip shot. He had not made a field goal of more than 40 yards all season, but he hit a 43-yarder in the first quarter and finished five-for-five, breaking a school record for field goals in a game.

There were other UVa heroes, including running back Tiki Barber, who scored a touchdown on the same field where his father, J.B., had played more than twenty years earlier for the Hokies. Tiki and his twin brother, defensive back Ronde, had not lived with their father since they were young children, but there was still a Tech graduate influence in their house—their mother, Geraldine. "I bit my tongue many times," says Geraldine, whose sons never considered the Hokies. "For obvious reasons, I had to stay out of it. You have to realize it's their life. [But] it's still my school and I want Tech to do well."

Nobody felt worse than DeShazo, who, as a redshirt freshman in 1989, mounted the goalpost after the

Below: **Nick Cullen celebrates a TD reception in Tech's 20-17 victory in 1993.** (Photo Jamie Stanek)

Elmo left and went to Virginia and I don't think they ever spoke again."

Come to think of it, maybe they haven't, Elmassian says. There's no grudge, according to Wiley, now living and working in The Plains, Virginia. He hasn't seen Elmassian or many of his old coaches because he doesn't arrange his schedule around football games. "I avoid crowds like the plague," says Wiley, who hasn't been to a Tech-UVa game since 1987, the last time he played in one.

Wiley almost went to Virginia, or at least he thought about it. He came from a private school

Mike Frederick brings down a Tech ball carrier. (Photo Frank Selden)

Hokies' 38-13 romp over Virginia in Lane Stadium. DeShazo had vowed to climb the goalpost following a 1994 victory, but he beat a hasty retreat after being victimized for five interceptions—two each by UVa defensive backs Percy Ellsworth and Joe Crocker, who was on his back when a deflected ball fell into his arms. "A tough day at the office," Tech coach Frank Beamer says. "Man, eight turnovers! I saw our players do things that I never have seen in practice."

They say that games like this are played for bragging rights and that certainly was the case in 1994, when the Tech-UVa game decided little else. The Hokies' fate was being determined more than 200 miles to the north, where West Virginia was beating Boston College 21-20, lifting the Hokies into at least a second-place tie in the Big East. Virginia, with a possible Fiesta Bowl appearance and a $3.5-million paycheck at stake, came back six days later and blew

background, but he wasn't always serious about his studies and, as a fifth-year student at Episcopal High School in Alexandria, his grade-point average dipped below the 2.0 required for a Division I scholarship. So, rather than lose a year of eligibility, Wiley found a school that did not field a football team, Flagler College in St. Augustine, Florida, and was able to transfer after one year.

Virginia remained in the picture until the admissions office suggested Wiley take a foreign language course, which swung the pendulum to the Hokies. He was a big, athletic, hard-nosed free safety who was

186   H O O S ' N ' H O K I E S • 1 0 0 Y E A R S O F V I R G I N I A / V I R G I N I A T E C H F O O T B A L L

So, nobody came away happy. Or, maybe they both came away happy. Never before had both teams gone to bowls in consecutive years. And at no point have both teams been successful at the same time.

It's been a long relationship. The seeds of disdain, planted a century ago, are deeply rooted.

Do Wahoos and Hokies still represent the bluebloods and the bumpkins? Probably not. The lines have been crossed and re-crossed, blurred through the years so that definite class distinctions no longer seem to exist. But the insults are real. So is the rivalry.

The Tech-Virginia game might not decide fates, and it might not always mean a whole lot in any football conference, but to the participants—the 'Hoos 'n' the Hokies—it's a fight for respect, a showdown that stirs up the Old Dominion like no other game.

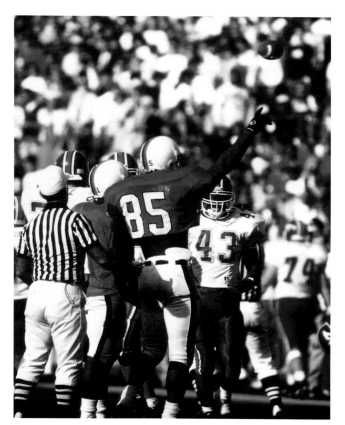

Above: Inspired by the comments of Will Furrer, Chris Slade had five sacks in 1991.
(Photo Frank Selden)

Left: Randy Neal's two interceptions against the Hokies were the first of his career.
(Photo David Greene)

a 19-7 third-quarter lead in losing to North Carolina State, 30-27.

This time, it was UVa that was headed to the Independence Bowl, where it beat Texas Christian 20-10, and Tech getting $1.5 million for playing in the Gator Bowl, where it would be routed by Tennessee 45-23. For the second year in a row, the loser in the Tech-UVa game had come away with the better bowl.

a major contributor for Dooley's last three teams, which went 24-10-1 from 1984-1986. No one was more critical of Tech's decision to dump Dooley than Wiley, whose career-long willingness to speak his mind didn't always endear him to the coaches.

"Elmassian would always get back at me by saying, 'You know what? You should have gone to Virginia.'" Wiley says. "He always said, 'You're at the wrong school. You're too much of a goddamn peacock and you're too much of a prep. You should have gone to UVa.' Any time I was feeling good about

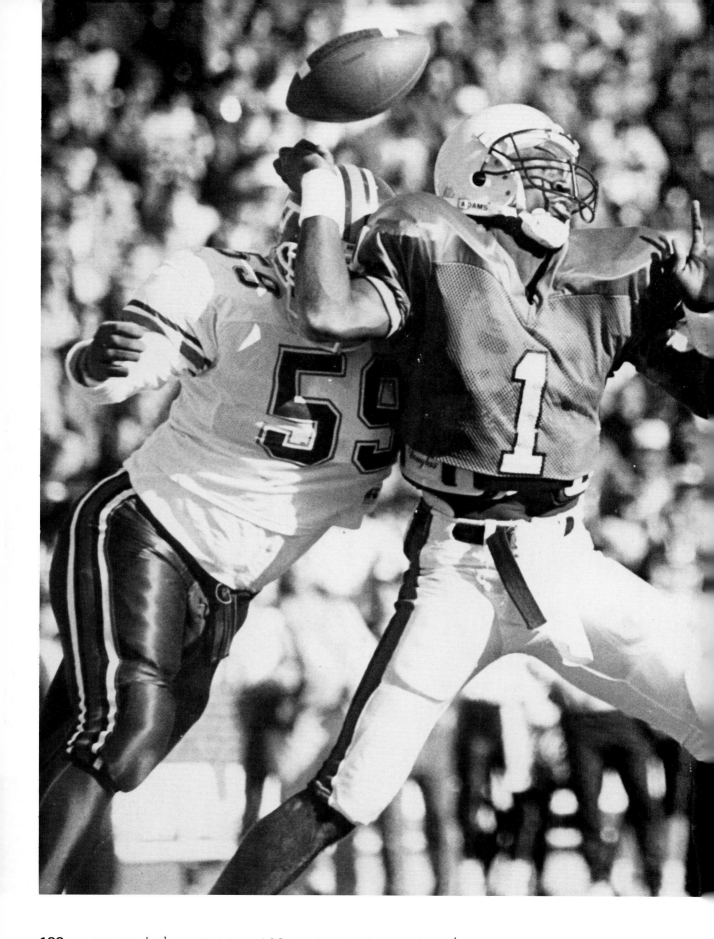

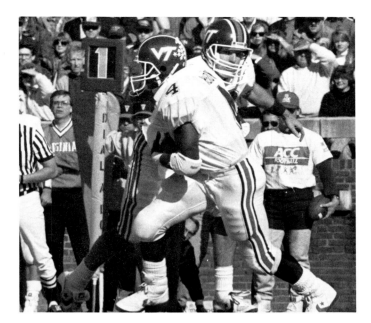

Opposite: J.C. Price forces a Symmion Willis fumble in 1993. (Photo Ruth Babylon)

Right: Vaughn Hebron gained 142 yards on 31 carries against the Cavaliers in 1990. (Photo Virginia Tech Sports Information)

Below: Antonio Freeman looks to avoid the Cavalier defense. (Photo Dave Knachel)

myself or had become a little ego-driven. Elmassian would insert that and try to deflate me.

—So then he takes the job at Virginia and he's trying to rationalize the move after telling us what lowlifes [the Cavaliers] were all those years. One of the last things I said to him was, 'Isn't this ironic, Coach? Now, you're the one who belongs at Virginia, not me.'"

Maurice DeShazo scrambles
downfield. (Photo Walker Nelms)

Shawn Moore

Below: Will Furrer and Jim Pyne.
(Photo Virginia Tech Sports Information)

Percy Ellsworth picked off two Hokie passes in 1994. (Photo Dan Grogan)

The Hokie Bird didn't have much to smile about after UVa came to town in 1994. (Photo Virginia Tech Sports Information)

UVa offensive lineman Tom Locklin and Tech defensive lineman J.C. Price (59) lock horns at the line of scrimmage. (Photo Dan Grogan)

Above left: Tech fullback Mark Poindexter barrels into the end zone. (Photo Bill Setliff)

Above right: Tyronne Drakeford picked off two passes against UVa as a freshman in 1990. (Virginia Tech Sports Information)

Right: Tech star guard Eugene Chung. (Photo Virginia Tech Sports Information)